Beautiful
BABY KNITS

LEOPARD

CONTENTS

CONTENTS

Cool cotton charmers in bright colours

Jack and Jill, page 70

ere is a superb collection of delightful knits for babies and toddlers. The range extends from warm woolly garments to ward off the winter cold to cooler cotton garments for summer days. There's something to please everyone: classic styles and interesting new designs, special occasion outfits and everyday garments, bold bright colours and soft pastels, simple easy-to-knit patterns and patterns for the more adventurous. With garments for the new baby right through to the three-year-old, the value of this book is outstanding. It will be with you for years.

HAND KNIT RATINGS

The patterns in *Beautiful Baby Knits* have been graded to help you choose the patterns suited to your knitting ability.

Easy knit   **For beginners**   **For advanced knitters**

Stars at the bottom of the circle suggest that an additional degree of patience is required for a quality finish.

QUANTITY AND CHOICE OF YARN

The quantities given in the patterns are approximate as they vary between knitters.
It is very important to use only the yarn specified in each pattern. Other yarns may give unsatisfactory results.

Looking good, feeling great in classic cream and white

Tommy Snooks and Bessie Brooks, page 49

Hold onto your hats, winter's on the way

Hey diddle diddle, page 38

EASY KNIT

Pretty pastels go hand in hand

Left: A pocketful of posies, page 73
Right: Like a teddy bear, page 76

Rub-a-dub-dub

EASY KNIT

The jacket and bonnet are knitted in a classic lacy pattern with matching bootees to complete the set

MEASUREMENTS
The jacket is designed to be a generous fit.

Size		A	B	C
Approx age	months	3	6	9
JACKET				
Fits underarm	cm	40	45	50
	ins	16	18	20
Garment measures	cm	44	50	55
Length (approx)	cm	26	29	32
Sleeve fits	cm	13	16	19
BONNET				
Length around face	cm	28	32	36
BOOTEES				
Length of foot (approx)	cm	8	9.5	11

MATERIALS
Patons 4 Ply Baby Wool 25 g balls

Jacket	5	5	6
Bonnet	1	1	1
Bootees	1	1	1

ACCESSORIES
1 pair each 3.25 mm (no. 10) and 2.75 mm (no. 12) Milward knitting needles, 3.25 mm (no. 10) circular needle or sizes needed to give correct tension, 3 buttons for Jacket, length of ribbon for Bonnet and Bootees.

TENSION
29 sts to 10 cm in width over stocking st, using 3.25 mm needles.
Please check your tension carefully. If less sts use smaller needles, if more sts use bigger needles.

Jacket

Worked in one piece to armholes.
Using 3.25 mm circular needle, cast on 213 (229, 245) sts.
Note A circular needle is recommended to accommodate the large number of sts. Do not join, work in rows.
Knit 4 rows garter st (1st row is wrong side).

Next row K12, ★ inc in next st, K3, rep from ★ to last 9 sts, K9... 261 (281, 301) sts.
1st row K5, P1, ★ yon, K1, sl 1, K1, psso, P3, K2 tog, K1, yrn, P1, rep from ★ to last 5 sts, K5.
2nd row K6, ★ P3, K3, P3, K1, rep from ★ to last 5 sts, K5.
3rd row K5, P2, ★ yon, K1, sl 1, K1, psso, P1, K2 tog, K1, yrn, P3, rep from

★ ending last rep with P2, K5 instead of P3.
4th row K7, P3, K1, P3, ★ K3, P3, K1, P3, rep from ★ to last 7 sts, K7.
5th row K5, P3, ★ yon, K1, sl 1, K2 tog, psso, K1, yrn, P5, rep from ★ ending last rep with P3, K5 instead of P5.
6th row K8, P5, ★ K5, P5, rep from ★ to last 8 sts, K8.
7th row K5, P4, ★ yon, sl 1, K2 tog, psso, yrn, P7, rep from ★ ending last rep with P4, K5 instead of P7.
8th row K9, P3, ★ K7, P3, rep from ★ to last 9 sts, K9.
9th row K5, P2, ★ K2 tog, K1, yrn, P1, yon, K1, sl 1, K1, psso, P3, rep from ★ ending last rep with P2, K5 instead of P3.
10th row As 4th row.
11th row K5, P1, ★ K2 tog, K1, yrn, P3, yon, K1, sl 1, K1, psso, P1, rep from ★ to last 5 sts, K5.
12th row As 2nd row.
13th row K5, K2 tog, ★ K1, yrn, P5, yon, K1, sl 1, K2 tog, psso, rep from ★ ending last rep with sl 1, K1, psso, K5 instead of sl 1, K2 tog, psso.

14th row K5, P3, K5, ★ P5, K5, rep from ★ to last 8 sts, P3, K5.
15th row K5, K2 tog, ★ yrn, P7, yon, sl 1, K2 tog, psso, rep from ★ ending last rep with sl 1, K1, psso, K5 instead of sl 1, K2 tog, psso.
16th row K5, P2, K7, ★ P3, K7, rep from ★ to last 7 sts, P2, K5.
Rows 1 to 16 incl form patt.
Cont in patt until work measures approx 14 (16, 18) cm from beg, ending with an 8th or 16th patt row.

Cont on last 34 (37, 41) sts for **Left Front**.

Next row K5, purl to end.

Keeping garter st border correct, dec at armhole edge in every row until 31 (34, 36) sts rem, then in alt row/s until 30 (32, 34) sts rem. Work 20 (18, 20) rows.

SHAPE NECK

Cast off 10 sts at beg of next row.

Dec at neck edge in next and alt rows until 16 (17, 19) sts rem.

Work 1 (3, 3) row/s stocking st.

SHAPE SHOULDER

Cast off 5 (6, 6) sts at beg of next row and foll alt row.

Work 1 row. Cast off.

Join yarn to next 63 (69, 77) sts for **Back**.

Purl 1 row.

Dec at each end of every row until 57 (63, 67) sts rem, then in alt row/s until 55 (59, 63) sts rem.

Work 29 (31, 33) rows stocking st.

SHAPE SHOULDERS

Cast off 5 (6, 6) sts at beg of next 4 rows, then 6 (5, 7) sts at beg of foll 2 rows.

Cast off rem 23 (25, 25) sts.

Join yarn to rem 34 (37, 41) sts for **Right Front** and work to correspond with Left Front, working a buttonhole (as before) in 14th rows from previous buttonhole twice... 3 buttonholes.

Sleeves

Using 3.25 mm needles, cast on 37 (39, 41) sts.

Knit 12 rows garter st (1st row is wrong side).

Next row K5 (2, 1), ★ inc in next st, K1 (2, 1), rep from ★ to last 4 (1, 0) st/s, K4 (1, 0)... 51 (51, 61) sts.

1st row P1, ★ yon, K1, sl 1, K1, psso, P3, K2 tog, K1, yrn, P1, rep from ★ to end.

2nd row K1, ★ P3, K3, P3, K1, rep from ★ to end.

3rd row P2, ★ yon, K1, sl 1, K1, psso, P1, K2 tog, K1, yrn, P3, rep from ★ ending last rep with P2 instead of P3.

Cont in patt as for Back, *as placed* in last 3 rows until work measures 13

Next row K6 (8, 8), ★ (K2 tog) 20 (9, 5) times, K1, rep from ★ to last 50 (26, 18) sts, (K2 tog) 22 (9, 5) times, knit to end... 139 (155, 171) sts.

Next row Knit.

Next row K2, y fwd, K2 tog (buttonhole), knit to end.

Knit 2 rows garter st.

Next row K5, purl to last 5 sts, K5.

DIVIDE FOR ARMHOLES

Next row K34 (37, 41), cast off 4 (6, 6) sts, K63 (69, 77), cast off 4 (6, 6) sts, knit to end.

(16, 19) cm from beg, working last row on wrong side.

SHAPE TOP
Cast off 2 (3, 3) sts at beg of next 2 rows.
Dec at each end of next and alt rows until 25 (17, 29) sts rem, then in every row until 11 sts rem. Cast off.

Collar

Using 3.25 mm needles, cast on 64 (72, 72) sts.
Knit 2 rows garter st (1st row is wrong side).
Next row K8, ★ inc in next st, K3, rep from ★ to last 4 sts, K4... 77 (87, 87) sts.
1st row: K3, P1, ★ yon, K1, sl 1, K1, psso, P3, K2 tog, K1, yrn, P1, rep from ★ to last 3 sts, K3.
2nd row K4, ★ P3, K3, P3, K1, rep from ★ to last 3 sts, K3.
3rd row K3, P2, ★ yon, K1, sl 1, K1, psso, P1, K2 tog, K1, yrn, P3, rep from ★ ending last rep with P2, K3 instead of P3.
Work a further 13 rows patt as for Back *as placed* in last 3 rows.
Knit 1 row.
Next row K5 (7, 7), ★ K2 tog, K7 (6, 6), rep from ★ to end... 69 (77, 77) sts.
Cast off 11 (13, 13) sts at beg of next 4 rows.
Cast off rem sts.

Make up

With a slightly damp cloth and warm iron, press lightly, taking care not to flatten patt. Using backstitch, join sleeve and shoulder seams. Sew in sleeves. Sew collar in position. Sew on buttons.

Bonnet

Using 2.75 mm needles, cast on 81 (91, 101) sts.
Knit 5 rows garter st (1st row is wrong side).
Change to 3.25 mm needles.
Work in patt as for Back of Jacket (omitting garter st edge) until work

measures approx 11 (12, 13) cm from beg, ending with an 8th or 16th patt row.

SHAPE BACK
1st row K7 (8, 9), sl 1, K2 tog, psso, ★ K13 (15, 17), sl 1, K2 tog, psso, rep from ★ to last 7 (8, 9) sts, knit to end.
Knit 3 rows garter st.
5th row K6 (7, 8), sl 1, K2 tog, psso, ★ K11 (13, 15), sl 1, K2 tog, psso, rep from ★ to last 6 (7, 8) sts, knit to end.
Knit 1 row.

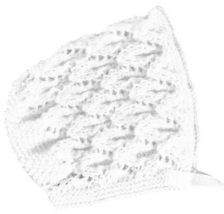

7th row K5 (6, 7), sl 1, K2 tog, psso, ★ K9 (11, 13), sl 1, K2 tog, psso, rep from ★ to last 5 (6, 7) sts, knit to end.
Cont dec 10 sts in this manner in alt rows until 11 sts rem.
Break off yarn, run end through rem sts, draw up firmly and fasten off securely.

Make up

With a slightly damp cloth and warm iron, press lightly, taking care not to flatten patt. Using a flat seam, join back seam. With right side facing and using 2.75 mm needles, knit up 65 (71, 77) sts evenly along lower edge of bonnet. Knit 6 rows garter st. Cast off. Sew on ribbon.

Bootees

Beg at top.
Using 3.25 mm needles, cast on 37 (41, 45) sts.
Knit 3 rows garter st (1st row is wrong side).

4th row Knit.
5th row K1, purl to last st, K1.
Rep 4th and 5th rows 9 (10, 11) times.
Next row K1, ★ y fwd, K2 tog, rep from ★ to end.
Next row Knit.

DIVIDE FOR INSTEP
Next row K24 (26, 28), *turn*.
Next row K11, *turn*.
Knit 16 (20, 24) rows garter st on these 11 sts.
Break off yarn.
With right side facing, join in yarn and knit up 9 (11, 13) sts evenly along side of instep, knit across 11 instep sts, knit up 9 (11, 13) sts evenly along other side of instep, knit to end... 55 (63, 71) sts.
Knit 7 (9, 11) rows garter st.

SHAPE FOOT
1st row [K1, K2 tog, K22 (26, 30), K2 tog] twice, K1.
2nd and alt rows Knit.
3rd row [K1, K2 tog, K20 (24, 28), K2 tog] twice, K1.
5th row [K1, K2 tog, K18 (22, 26), K2 tog] twice, K1.
7th row [K1, K2 tog, K16 (20, 24), K2 tog] twice, K1.
9th row [K1, K2 tog, K14 (18, 22), K2 tog] twice, K1... 35 (43, 51) sts.
Cast off *loosely*.

Make up

With a slightly damp cloth and warm iron, press lightly, taking care not to flatten patt. Using a flat seam, join leg and foot seams. Thread ribbon through holes at ankle.

Bye, baby bunting

Garter and moss stitch feature in this versatile, easy-to-knit outfit of cardigan, leggings and bootees

MEASUREMENTS

The cardigan is designed to be a generous fit.

Size		A	B	C	D
Approx age	months	0	3	6	12
CARDIGAN					
Fits underarm	cm	35	40	45	50
	ins	14	16	18	20
Garment measures	cm	39	44.5	50	55.5
Length	cm	20	24	27	30
Sleeve fits	cm	11	13	16	19
LEGGINGS					
Length	cm	26	29	34	39
BOOTEES					
Length of foot (approx)	cm	7	8	9.5	11

MATERIALS

Patons 3 Ply Baby Wool 25 g balls

Cardigan	2	3	3	4
Leggings	2	3	3	4
Bootees	1	1	1	1

ACCESSORIES

1 pair each 3.25 mm (no. 10), 3.00 mm (no. 11) and 2.75 mm (no. 12) Milward knitting needles or sizes needed to give correct tension, 4 (5, 6, 6) buttons for Cardigan, length of round elastic for Leggings, length of ribbon for Bootees.

TENSION

30 sts to 10 cm in width over moss st, using 3.25 mm needles.
Please check your tension carefully. If less sts use smaller needles, if more sts use bigger needles.

Cardigan

Back

Using 3.25 mm needles, cast on 57 (65, 73, 81) sts.
Knit 7 rows garter st (1st row is wrong side), inc 4 sts evenly across last row… 61 (69, 77, 85) sts.
8th row K1, ★ P1, K1, rep from ★ to end.

Last row forms moss st patt.
Work in moss st until work measures 11 (14, *16*, 18) cm from beg, working last row on wrong side.
Tie a coloured thread at each end of last row to mark beg of armholes as there is no armhole shaping.
Work a further 40 (44, *50*, 54) rows patt.

SHAPE SHOULDERS

Keeping patt correct, cast off 5 (5, 6, 7) sts at beg of next 6 rows, then 3 (7, 7, 7) sts at beg of foll 2 rows.
Cast off rem 25 (25, 27, 29) sts.

Left Front

Using 3.25 mm needles, cast on 29 (33, 37, 41) sts.
Knit 7 rows garter st, inc 2 sts evenly across last row… 31 (35, 39, 43) sts.
Work in moss st until work measures 11 (14, *16*, 18) cm from beg, working last row on wrong side.
Tie a coloured thread at end of last row to mark beg of armhole.
Work a further 24 (28, *34*, 36) rows patt.

SHAPE NECK

Next row Patt 24 (28, *32*, 36), *turn* and leave rem 7 sts on a safety pin.
Dec at neck edge in alt rows until 18 (21, *25*, 28) sts rem.
Work 3 (1, *1*, 1) row/s patt.

SHAPE SHOULDER

Keeping patt correct, cast off 5 (5, 6, 7) sts at beg of next and alt rows 3 times in all.
Work 1 row. Cast off.

Right Front

Work to correspond with Left Front.

Sleeves

Using 3.25 mm needles, cast on 40 (44, 46, 50) sts.
Knit 7 rows garter st (1st row is wrong side), inc once in centre of last row… 41 (45, 47, 51) sts.
Work in patt as for Back, inc at each end of 5th and foll 10th (8th, *8th*, 10th) rows until there are 47 (55, 59, 65) sts.
Cont without shaping until work measures 9 (11, *14*, 17) cm from beg, working last row on wrong side.
Cast off 4 (4, 5, 5) sts at beg of next 8 rows. Cast off rem sts.

Neckband

Using backstitch, join shoulder seams.
With right side facing and using 3.25 mm needles, knit up 80 (80, 84, 88) sts evenly around neck, incl sts from safety pins.
Knit 6 rows garter st. Cast off *loosely.*

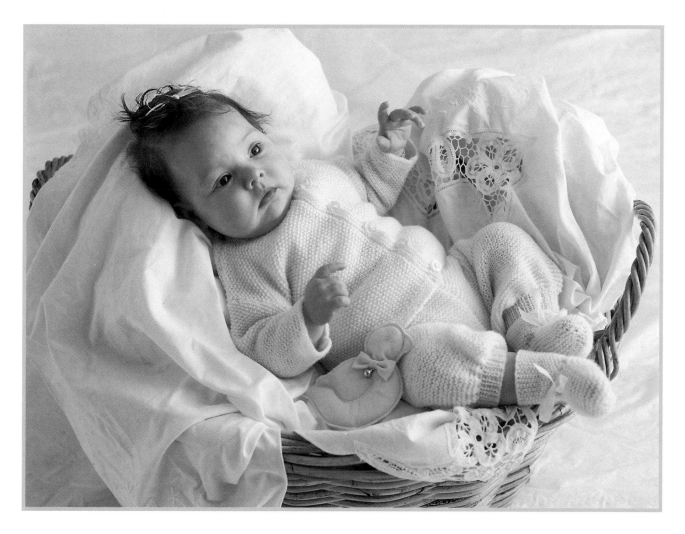

Right Front Band

Using 3.25 mm needles, cast on 52 (62, 75, 80) sts.

Knit 2 rows garter st.

3rd row K4, ★ y fwd, K2 tog (buttonhole), K12 (11, *11*, 12), rep from ★ 2 (3, *4*, 4) times, y fwd, K2 tog, K4... 4 (5, *6*, 6) buttonholes.

Knit 3 rows garter st. Cast off *loosely*.

Left Front Band

Work as for Right Front Band, omitting buttonholes.

Make up

With a slightly damp cloth and warm iron, press lightly, taking care not to flatten patt. Using backstitch, join sleeve and side seams to coloured threads. Sew in sleeves. Sew front bands in position. Sew on buttons. Press seams.

Leggings

Legs

Both alike, beg at ankle.

Using 2.75 mm needles, cast on 41 (45, *49*, 51) sts.

1st row K2, ★ P1, K1, rep from ★ to last st, K1.

2nd row K1, ★ P1, K1, rep from ★ to end.

Rep 1st and 2nd rows 5 times, then 1st row once.

14th row Rib 5 (5, 7, 5), inc in each st to last 6 sts, rib 6... 71 (79, 85, 91) sts.

Change to 3.25 mm needles.

Knit in garter st until work measures 11 (13, *17*, 21) cm from beg, working last row on wrong side.

SHAPE CROTCH

Cast on 2 (2, 3, 3) sts at beg of next 2 rows... 75 (83, *91*, 97) sts.

Dec at each end of 7th (9th, *7th*, 9th) and foll 12th (12th, *12th*, 14th) rows until 61 (69, 75, 83) sts rem.

Knit a further 7 (9, *5*, 9) rows garter st.

Work 14 rows rib as before. Cast off *loosely* in rib.

Make up

With a slightly damp cloth and warm iron, press lightly. Using backstitch, join front, back and leg seams. Thread round elastic through 1st, 7th and 14th rows of waistband and draw up to desired measurement.

Bootees

Beg at sole.

Using 3.25 mm needles, cast on 25 (35, *45*, 55) sts.

Continued on page 109

Hush-a-bye baby

A delightful combination of overalls and jumper in soft wool for the baby who arrives in the cooler months

MEASUREMENTS

The jumper is designed to be a generous fit.

Size		A	B	C	D
Approx age	months	3	6	12	18
Fits underarm	cm	40	45	50	52.5
	ins	16	18	20	21
OVERALLS					
Overalls measure	cm	42	47.5	52.5	55.5
Length	cm	44	51	58	65
JUMPER					
Jumper measures	cm	43	48	54	57
Length	cm	21	24	28	30.5
Sleeve fits	cm	13	16	19	21

MATERIALS

Patons 3 Ply Baby Wool 25 g balls

Overalls	3	4	4	5
Jumper	2	3	3	4

ACCESSORIES

1 pair each 3.25 mm (no. 10) and 2.75 mm (no. 12) Milward knitting needles, 2.75 mm (no. 12) circular needle or sizes needed to give correct tension, 1 stitch holder and 2 buttons for Overalls 2 stitch holders and 3 buttons for Jumper.

TENSION

30 sts and 48.5 rows to 10 cm over moss st, using 3.25 mm needles for yoke of Overalls. 31 sts and 41 rows to 10 cm over stocking st, using 3.25 mm needles for Overalls and Jumper.
Please check your tension carefully. If less sts use smaller needles, if more sts use bigger needles.

Overalls

Right Leg

Using 2.75 mm needles, cast on 43 (47, 51, 55) sts.
1st row K2, ★ P1, K1, rep from ★ to last st, K1.
2nd row K1, ★ P1, K1, rep from ★ to end.

Rep 1st and 2nd rows 5 (6, 6, 7) times, then 1st row once.
Next row Rib 2 (2, 0, 1), inc in each st to last 3 (1, 1, 1) st/s, rib 3 (1, 1, 1)... 81 (91, 101, 108) sts.
Change to 3.25 mm needles.
Work in stocking st, inc at each end of 5th and foll 6th (6th, 8th, 10th) rows until there are 93 (97, 117, 124) sts.

Size B only, then in foll 8th rows until there are 105 sts. **All sizes**, work 7 (7, 11, 11) rows. ★★
Leave sts on a stitch holder.

Left Leg

Work as for Right Leg to ★★.
Next row Cast on 4 sts, *turn*, knit to end, *turn*, cast on 6 sts, knit across right leg sts, *turn*, cast on 4 sts... 200 (224, 248, 262) sts.
Note If this number of sts will not fit comfortably on needle, we suggest using a circular needle.
Cont in stocking st until work measures 16 (17, 18, 19) cm from where legs were joined, ending with a purl row.
Next row K6 (6, 6, 4), ★ K2 tog, K1, rep from ★ to last 5 (5, 5, 3) sts, K5 (5, 5, 3)... 137 (153, 169, 177) sts.
Change to 2.75 mm needles.
Work 15 rows rib as for cuff, beg with a 2nd row.
Change to 3.25 mm needles.

BEG MOSS ST PATT

1st row K1, ★ P1, K1, rep from ★ to end.
Last row forms moss st patt for rem.
Work 1 row.

DIVIDE FOR ARMHOLES

Next row Patt 29 (31, 33, 35), cast off 11 (15, 19, 19) sts, patt 57 (61, 65, 69), cast off 11 (15, 19, 19) sts, patt to end.
Cont on last 29 (31, 33, 35) sts for **Right back**.
Dec at armhole edge in alt rows until 24 (26, 27, 29) sts rem.
Work 30 (38, 44, 50) rows patt.

SHAPE NECK

Cast off 10 (12, 13, 15) sts at beg of next row... 14 sts.
Dec at neck edge in every row until 9 sts rem.
Work 13 (15, 15, 17) rows, dec at each end of last 2 rows... 5 sts.
Cast off.
With wrong side facing, join yarn to next 57 (61, 65, 69) sts for **Front**.
Dec at each end of alt rows until 47 (51, 53, 57) sts rem.
Work 13 (21, 25, 31) rows patt.

SHAPE NECK

Next row Patt 15 (16, *16*, 17), *turn* and cont on these sts.

Dec at neck edge in alt rows until 9 sts rem.

Work 13 (13, *15*, 15) rows patt.

Next row Patt 4, yrn, P2 tog, patt 3... buttonhole.

Work 3 rows, dec at each end of last 2 rows... 5 sts.

Cast off *in moss st.*

Slip next 17 (19, *21*, 23) sts onto stitch holder and leave. Join yarn to rem sts and work other side to correspond.

With wrong side facing, join yarn to rem 29 (31, *33*, 35) sts for **Left Back** and work to correspond with Right Back.

Armhole and Neckband

With right side facing and using 2.75 mm circular needle, knit up 22 (26, *27*, 31) sts around Left Back edge to top of back strap, 10 sts across strap, 86 (104, *120*, 132) sts around armhole edge to top of left front strap, 10 sts across strap, 57 (63, *67*, 73) sts around front neck edge to top of right front strap (dec once in centre of stitch holder), 10 sts across strap, 86 (104, *120*, 132) sts around armhole edge to top of back strap, 10 sts across strap, then 22 (26, *27*, 31) sts around Right Back edge... 313 (363, *401*, 439) sts. Work 7 rows rib, beg with a 2nd row. Cast off *loosely* in rib.

Make up

With a slightly damp cloth and warm iron, press lightly, taking care not to flatten patt. Using backstitch, join centre back and leg seams. Fold armhole and neckband in half onto wrong side and slipstitch in position. Sew on buttons. Press seams.

Jumper

Back

Using 2.75 mm needles, cast on 69 (77, *85*, 91) sts.

1st row K2, ★ P1, K1, rep from ★ to last st, K1.

2nd row K1, ★ P1, K1, rep from ★ to end.

Rep 1st and 2nd rows 5 times... 12 rows rib in all.

Change to 3.25 mm needles.

Work in stocking st until work measures 11 (13, *15*, 17) cm from beg, ending with a purl row.

SHAPE ARMHOLES

Cast off 2 (3, *3*, 3) sts at beg of next 2 rows.

Dec at each end of next and alt rows until 61 (67, *75*, 79) sts rem. ★★

Work 17 (21, *29*, 29) rows.

DIVIDE FOR BACK OPENING

Next row K33 (36, *40*, 42), *turn* and cont on these sts.

2nd row K5, purl to end.

3rd row Knit.

Rep 2nd and 3rd rows twice, then 2nd row once.

9th row Knit to last 3 sts, y fwd, K2 tog (buttonhole), K1.

Rep 2nd and 3rd rows 5 times, then 2nd row once, working a buttonhole (as before) in 10th row from previous buttonhole.

SHAPE SHOULDER

Cast off 5 (6, *7*, 8) sts at beg of next row and foll alt row, then 6 (6, *7*, 7) sts at beg of foll alt row.

Work 1 row.

Leave rem 17 (18, *19*, 19) sts on a stitch holder.

Join yarn to rem sts, cast on 5 sts for garter st underlap and work to correspond with other side, omitting buttonholes.

Front

Work as for Back to ★★.

Work 21 (25, *31*, 31) rows.

SHAPE NECK

Next row K23 (25, *29*, 31), *turn* and cont on these sts.

Dec at neck edge in alt rows until 16 (18, *21*, 23) sts rem.

Work 1 row.

SHAPE SHOULDER

Cast off 5 (6, *7*, 8) sts at beg of next row and foll alt row.

Work 1 row. Cast off.

Slip next 15 (17, *17*, 17) sts onto stitch holder and leave. Join yarn to rem sts and work other side to correspond.

Sleeves

Using 2.75 mm needles, cast on 39 (41, *43*, 47) sts.

Work 12 rows rib as for Back, inc 6 sts evenly across last row... 45 (47, *49*, 53) sts.

Change to 3.25 mm needles.

Work 4 rows stocking st.

5th row K2, "M1", knit to last 2 sts, "M1", K2.

Cont in stocking st, inc (as before) at each end of foll 6th (8th, *8th*, 10th) rows until there are 55 (57, *61*, 65) sts. Cont without shaping until work measures 13 (16, *19*, 21) cm from beg, ending with a purl row.

SHAPE TOP

Cast off 2 sts at beg of next 2 rows.

Dec at each end of next and alt rows until 35 (35, *31*, 37) sts rem, then in every row until 9 sts rem. Cast off.

Continued on page 109

Twinkle, twinkle

MEASUREMENTS

The jacket is designed to be a generous fit.

Size		**A**	**B**	**C**
Approx age	months	3	6	12
JACKET				
Fits underarm	cm	40	45	50
	ins	16	18	20
Garment measures	cm	44	50	55
Length	cm	23	26	30
Sleeve fits	cm	13	16	19
HAT				
Fits head	cm	40	45	48

MATERIALS

Patons 4 Ply Baby Wool 25 g balls

Jacket	3	3	4
Hat	1	1	1

A simple outfit made surprisingly special by the addition of pretty braid to the jacket and hat

ACCESSORIES

1 pair each 3.25 mm (no. 10) and 2.75 mm (no. 12) Milward knitting needles or sizes needed to give correct tension, 2.2 (2.4, 2.6) metres braid, 1 button for Jacket.

TENSION

29 sts to 10 cm in width over stocking st, using 3.25 mm needles.
Please check your tension carefully. If less sts use smaller needles, if more sts use bigger needles.

Jacket

Back

Using 3.25 mm needles, cast on 61 (71, 79) sts.

Knit 7 rows garter st (1st row is wrong side), inc 4 sts evenly across last row ... 65 (75, 83) sts.

Work in stocking st until work measures 12.5 (14.5, 17) cm from beg, ending with a purl row.

Tie a coloured thread at each end of last row to mark beg of armholes as there is no armhole shaping.

Work a further 38 (42, 48) rows stocking st.

SHAPE SHOULDERS

Cast off 6 (8, 9) sts at beg of next 4 rows, then 7 (7, 8) sts at beg of foll 2 rows.

Cast off rem 27 (29, 31) sts.

Left Front

Using 3.25 mm needles, cast on 31 (36, 40) sts.

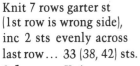

Knit 7 rows garter st (1st row is wrong side), inc 2 sts evenly across last row ... 33 (38, 42) sts.

8th row Knit.

9th row K4, purl to end.

Keeping garter st border correct, cont in stocking st until work measures 12.5 (14.5, 17) cm from beg, ending with a 9th row.

Tie a coloured thread at end of last row to mark beg of armhole.

Work a further 20 (24, 28) rows stocking st.

SHAPE NECK

Next row K27 (30, 34), *turn* and leave rem 6 (8, 8) sts on a safety pin.

Dec at neck edge in alt rows until 19 (23, 26) sts rem.

Work 1 (3, 3) row/s.

SHAPE SHOULDER

Cast off 6 (8, 9) sts at beg of next row and foll alt row.

Work 1 row. Cast off.

Right Front

Work to correspond with Left Front.

Sleeves

Using 3.25 mm needles, cast on 43 (47, 49) sts.

Knit 7 rows garter st (1st row is wrong side).

Work 4 rows stocking st.

12th row K2, "M1", knit to last 2 sts, "M1", K2.

Cont in stocking st, inc (as before) at each end of foll 4th rows until there are 55 (61, 69) sts.

Cont without shaping until work measures 11 (14, 17) cm from beg, ending with a purl row.

Cast off 4 (5, 6) sts at beg of next 10 rows. Cast off rem sts *loosely*.

Neckband

Using backstitch, join shoulder seams. With right side facing, slip sts from right front safety pin onto a 2.75 mm needle. Using same needle knit up 68 (72, 76) sts evenly around neck, incl sts on left front safety pin ... 74 (80, 84) sts.

Knit 6 rows garter st. Cast off *loosely*.

Make up

With a slightly damp cloth and warm iron, press lightly. Using backstitch, join sleeve and side seams to coloured threads. Sew in sleeves. Sew braid on right side around all edges of jacket and sleeves (over garter st edge), mitring at corners. Make buttonloop at neck edge and sew on button to correspond. Press seams.

Hat

Using 2.75 mm needles, cast on 117 (133, 141) sts.

1st row K2, ★ P1, K1, rep from ★ to last st, K1.

2nd row K1, ★ P1, K1, rep from ★ to end.

Rep 1st and 2nd rows 5 times ... 12 rows rib in all.

Change to 3.25 mm needles.

Work in stocking st until work measures 13 (14, 15) cm from beg, ending with a purl row.

Next row K1, ★ K2 tog, rep from ★ to end ... 59 (67, 71) sts.

Break off yarn, run end through rem sts, draw up and fasten off securely.

Make up

With a slightly damp cloth and warm iron, press lightly. Using backstitch, join seam. Cut a 12 cm length of braid for loop, fold in half and slip ends through top of hat, sew raw edges to inside of hat. Sew braid around hat just above rib. Press seam.

Ring o'roses

Tiny grub roses adorn the yoke of this sweet little dress knitted with long sleeves in wool or with short sleeves in cotton

MEASUREMENTS

The dress is designed to be a generous fit.

Size		A	B	C
Approx age	months	3	6	12
DRESS				
Fits underarm	cm	40	45	50
	ins	16	18	20
Length	cm	34	38	43
Sleeve fits (long)	cm	13	16	19
(short)	cm	4	4	4
SHOES				
Length of foot (approx)	cm	8	9.5	11

MATERIALS

Patons 4 Ply Baby Wool 25 g balls

Dress (long sleeves)	6	7	7
(short sleeves)	5	6	6
Shoes	1	1	1

Or Patons 4 Ply Gem Cotton 50 g balls

Dress (long sleeves)	5	5	6
(short sleeves)	4	4	5
Shoes	1	1	1

ACCESSORIES

For Baby Wool   1 pair each 3.25 mm (no. 10) and 2.75 mm (no. 12) Milward knitting needles, 3.25 mm (no. 10) circular needle or sizes needed to give correct tension. **For Gem**   1 pair each 2.75 mm (no. 12) and 2.00 mm (no. 14) Milward knitting needles, 2.75 mm (no. 12) circular needle, or sizes needed to give correct tension.

5 stitch holders and 4 buttons for Dress, 2 buttons for Shoes, Anchor Stranded Cotton in Dark Pink, Medium Pink, Pale Pink and Soft Green (shades 068, 75, 049 and 0261).

TENSION

29 sts to 10 cm in width over stocking st, using 3.25 mm needles and Baby Wool, or 2.75 mm needles and Gem.

Please check your tension carefully. If less sts use smaller needles, if more sts use bigger needles.

Note   Instructions are written for **Baby Wool**. If garments are knitted in **Gem** use 2.75 mm needles in place of 3.25 mm and 2.00 mm needles in place of 2.75 mm.

Dress

Back

Using 2.75 mm needles, cast on 119 (*135, 151*) sts.

Work 6 rows stocking st.

7th row (hem edge)   K1, ★ y fwd, K2 tog, rep from ★ to end.

Work 7 rows stocking st (beg with a purl row).

Change to 3.25 mm needles.

Work in stocking st until work measures 22 (*25, 29*) cm from *row of holes* at hem edge, ending with a purl row.

Tie a coloured thread at each end of last row to mark beg of armholes as there is no armhole shaping. ★★

Work 6 (*10, 14*) rows stocking st.

DIVIDE FOR BACK OPENING

1st row   K62 (*70, 78*), *turn and cont* on these sts.

2nd row   K5, purl to end.

3rd row   Knit.

Rep 2nd and 3rd rows twice.

8th row   K5, ★ P2 tog, rep from ★ to last st, P1 ... 34 (*38, 42*) sts.

Leave these sts on a stitch holder.

Join yarn to rem sts, cast on 5 sts for underlap, knit to end.

Cont on these 62 (*70, 78*) sts.

2nd row   Purl to last 5 sts, K5.

3rd row Knit.

Rep 2nd and 3rd rows twice.

8th row P1, ★ P2 tog, rep from ★ to last 5 sts, K5... 34 (38, 42) sts.

Leave these sts on a stitch holder.

Front

Work as for Back to ★★.

Work 13 (17, 21) rows stocking st.

Next row P3, ★ P2 tog, rep from ★ to last 4 sts, P4... 63 (71, 79) sts.

Leave these sts on a stitch holder.

Long Sleeves

Using 2.75 mm needles, cast on 35 (37, 39) sts.

Work 6 rows stocking st.

7th row (hem edge) K1, ★ y fwd, K2 tog, rep from ★ to end.

Work 7 rows stocking st (beg with a purl row), inc 8 sts evenly across last row... 43 (45, 47) sts.

Change to 3.25 mm needles.

Work 4 rows stocking st.

5th row K2, "M1", knit to last 2 sts, "M1", K2.

Cont in stocking st, inc (as before) at each end of foll 4th (4th, 6th) rows until there are 59 (51, 61) sts. **Sizes B and C only**, then in foll (6th, 8th) rows until there are (61, 65) sts. **All sizes**, cont without shaping until work measures 13 (16, 19) cm from *row of holes* at hem, ending with a purl row.

Tie a coloured thread at each end of last row to mark end of sleeve seam.

Work 13 (17, 21) rows stocking st.

Next row P0 (1, 0), ★ P2 tog, P2, rep from ★ to last 3 (4, 5) sts, P2 tog, P1 (2, 1), (P2 tog) 0 (0, 1) time/s... 44 (46, 48) sts.

Leave these sts on a stitch holder.

Short Sleeves

Using 2.75 mm needles, cast on 45 (47, 51) sts.

Work 6 rows stocking st.

7th row (hem edge) K1, ★ y fwd, K2 tog, rep from ★ to end.

Work 6 rows stocking st.

14th row P2 (2, 6), ★ inc in next st (purlways), P2, rep from ★ to last 1 (3, 3) st/s, P1 (3, 3)... 59 (61, 65) sts.

Change to 3.25 mm needles.

Work in stocking st until work measures 4 cm from *row of holes* at hem, ending with a purl row.

Tie a coloured thread at each end of last row to mark end of sleeve seam.

Work 13 (17, 21) rows stocking st.

Next row P0 (1, 0), ★ P2 tog, P2, rep from ★ to last 3 (4, 5) sts, P2 tog, P1 (2, 1), (P2 tog) 0 (0, 1) time/s... 44 (46, 48) sts.

Leave these sts on a stitch holder.

Yoke

Using backstitch, join sleeves to Back and Front above coloured threads. Slip all sts from stitch holders onto 3.25 mm circular needle... 219 (239, 259) sts.

1st and 2nd rows Beg with right side facing, knit.

3rd row Knit to last 3 sts, y fwd, K2 tog, K1... buttonhole.

4th and 5th rows Knit.

6th row K5, purl to last 5 sts, K5.

Rep 5th and 6th rows twice.

11th row K12, ★ (K2 tog, K5) twice, K2 tog, K4, rep from ★ to last 7 sts, K7... 189 (206, 223) sts.

Rep 6th row once, then 5th and 6th rows once.

Rep rows 1 to 4 incl once.

19th row K11, ★ (K2 tog, K4) twice, K2 tog, K3, rep from ★ to last 8 sts, K8... 159 (173, 187) sts.

Rep 6th row once, then 5th and 6th rows 3 times.

27th row K11, ★ (K2 tog, K3) twice, K2 tog, K2, rep from ★ to last 8 sts, K8... 129 (140, 151) sts.

28th row As 6th row.

Rep rows 1 to 5 incl once.

34th row As 6th row.

35th row K10, ★ (K2 tog, K2) twice, K2 tog, K1, rep from ★ to last 9 sts, K9... 99 (107, 115) sts.

Rep 6th row once, then 5th and 6th rows 3 times.

43rd row K6 (8, 5), ★ K2 tog, K2, K2 tog, K2 (1, 1), rep from ★ to last 5 (8, 5) sts, K5 (8, 5)... 77 (81, 85) sts.

44th row As 6th row.

Change to 2.75 mm needles for **Neckband**.

1st row K5 (9, 6), ★ K2 tog, K7 (7, 8), rep from ★ to last 9 sts, K2 tog, K4, y fwd, K2 tog, K1... 69 (73, 77) sts.

2nd row K5, purl to last 5 sts, K5.

3rd row Knit.

Rep 2nd and 3rd rows once, then 2nd row once.

7th row Cast off 5 sts, K1 (st left on needle after casting off), ★ y fwd, K2 tog, rep from ★ to last 5 sts, K5.

8th row Cast off 5 sts, purl to end... 59 (63, 67) sts. Work 4 rows stocking st. Cast off *loosely*.

Make up

With a slightly damp cloth and warm iron, press lightly. Using backstitch, join side and sleeve seams. Fold neckband, cuffs and hem onto wrong side at row of holes and slipstitch in position. Sew underlap in position. Sew on buttons. Work Grub Roses in Bullion Stitch on yoke as illustrated below, using Dark Pink in centre, then Medium Pink, then Pale Pink at outer edge. Work 2 leaves on each side of each rose. Press seams and hems.

BULLION STITCH AND GRUB ROSE

Pick up a backstitch, the size of the Bullion Stitch required, bringing the needle point out where it first emerged, do not pull the needle right through the fabric. Twist the thread round the needle point as many times as required to equal the space of the backstitch. Hold the left thumb on the coiled thread and pull the needle through; still holding the coiled thread, turn the needle back to where it was inserted (see arrow) and insert in same place. Pull thread through until the Bullion Stitch lies flat. Use

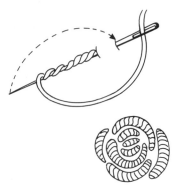

a needle with a small eye to allow the thread to pass through the coils easily. Arrange a circular group of Bullion Stitches to make a Grub Rose.

Shoes

Using 3.25 mm needles, cast on 35 (45, 55) sts.

1st and alt rows (wrong side) Knit.

2nd row K1, ★ "M1", K16 (21, 26), "M1", K1, rep from ★ once.

4th row K1, ★ "M1", K18 (23, 28), "M1", K1, rep from ★ once.

6th row K1, ★ "M1", K20 (25, 30), "M1", K1, rep from ★ once.

8th row K1, ★ "M1", K22 (27, 32), "M1", K1, rep from ★ once.

10th row K1, ★ "M1", K24 (29, 34), "M1", K1, rep from ★ once... 55 (65, 75) sts.

11th and 12th rows Knit.

13th row K1, purl to last st, K1.

Rep 12th and 13th rows 2 (3, 4) times.

SHAPE INSTEP

1st row K30 (35, 40), sl 1, K1, psso, K1, *turn*.

2nd row P7, P2 tog, P1, *turn*.

3rd row K8, sl 1, K1, psso, K1, *turn*.

4th row P9, P2 tog, P1, *turn*.

5th row K10, sl 1, K1, psso, *turn*.

6th row P10, P2 tog, *turn*.

7th row K10, sl 1, K1, psso, *turn*.

Rep 6th and 7th rows 1 (2, 3) time/s, then 6th row once.

Next row Knit to end... 45 (53, 61) sts.

Next row Knit.

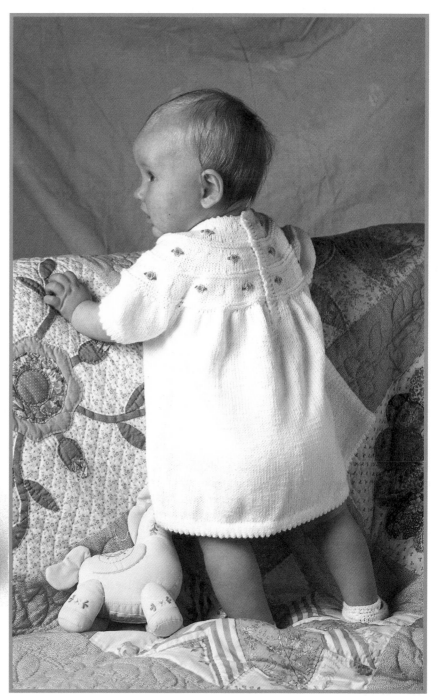

Next row K16 (20, 24), K2 tog, K9, sl 1, K1, psso, K16 (20, 24). Cast off knitways.

Straps

Using 3.25 mm needles, cast on 35 (38, 41) sts.

1st row (wrong side) Knit.

2nd row K2, y fwd, K2 tog (button-hole), knit to end.

Cast off *loosely* knitways.

Make up

With a slightly damp cloth and warm iron, press lightly. Using a flat seam, join back and foot seams. Sew centre of strap to back of shoe for 2 cm each side of seam (taking care to reverse strap on second shoe so that button-hole is at other end). Sew on buttons. Press seams. Embroider with a single rose and 2 leaves as illustrated.

Pretty maid

Every little girl will look adorable in this full skirted dress with its detachable fabric and lace collar. Use the same fabric to trim the blanket for that totally coordinated look

MEASUREMENTS

This garment is designed to be a generous fit.

Size		A	B	C	D
Approx age	months	3	6	12	18
Fits underarm	cm	40	45	50	52.5
	ins	16	18	20	21
Length	cm	35	39	44	49
Sleeve fits	cm	13	16	19	21

MATERIALS

Patons Gem Cotton 4 Ply 50 g balls	5	5	6	6

ACCESSORIES

1 pair each 2.75 mm (no. 12) and 2.00 mm (no. 14) Milward knitting needles or sizes needed to give correct tension, 3 buttons.

For Collar 60 cm square of Liberty fabric (we used fabric no. 332022.M), 80 cm of pre-gathered lace, a small flat button (or if preferred use a purchased collar).

TENSION

29 sts to 10 cm in width over stocking st, using 2.75 mm needles.

Please check your tension carefully. If less sts use smaller needles, if more sts use bigger needles.

Back

Using 2.00 mm needles, cast on 145 (169, *185*, 193) sts.

Work 6 rows stocking st.

Next row K1, ★ y fwd, K2 tog, rep from ★ to end.

Work 7 rows stocking st.

Change to 2.75 mm needles.

BEG PATT

1st row K4, ★ P1, K7, rep from ★ to last 5 sts, P1, K4.

2nd row P3, ★ K1, P1, K1, P5, rep from ★ to last 6 sts, K1, P1, K1, P3.

3rd row K2, ★ P1, K3, rep from ★ to last 3 sts, P1, K2.

4th row P1, ★ K1, P5, K1, P1, rep from ★ to end.

5th row ★ P1, K7, rep from ★ to last st, P1.

6th row As 4th row.

7th row As 3rd row.

8th row As 2nd row.

Last 8 rows form patt.

Cont in patt until work measures 23 (26, *29*, 33.5) cm from eyelet row, working last row on right side.

Next row (P2 tog) 22 (22, *23*, 28) times, (P3 tog) 19 (27, *31*, 27) times, (P2 tog) 22 (22, *23*, 28) times... 63 (71, 77, 83) sts.

Work 8 rows stocking st.

SHAPE ARMHOLES

Cast off 4 (5, 6, 7) sts at beg of next 2 rows... 55 (61, *65*, 69) sts. ★★

Work a further 0 (4, *12*, 14) rows stocking st.

DIVIDE FOR BACK OPENING

1st row K30 (33, *35*, 37), *turn* and cont on these sts.

2nd row K5, purl to end.

3rd row Knit.

Rep 2nd and 3rd rows 4 times, then 2nd row once.

13th row Knit to last 3 sts, y fwd, K2 tog (buttonhole), K1.

Rep rows 2 to 13 incl once, 2nd and 3rd rows 5 times, then 2nd row once.

SHAPE SHOULDER

Next row Cast off 6 (6, 7, 7) sts, knit to last 3 sts, y fwd, K2 tog, K1.

Cast off 6 (6, 7, 7) sts at beg of foll alt row, then 5 (7, 6, 8) sts at beg of foll alt row.

Work 1 row. Cast off rem 13 (14, *15*, 15) sts.

Join yarn to rem sts, cast on 5 sts for underlap, knit to end.

Work to correspond with other side, omitting buttonholes.

Front

Work as for Back to ★★.

Work a further 20 (24, *30*, 32) rows stocking st.

SHAPE NECK

Next row K22 (25, *26*, 28), cast off 11 (11, *13*, 13) sts, knit to end.

Cont on last 22 (25, *26*, 28) sts.

Dec at neck edge in alt rows until 17 (19, *20*, 22) sts rem.

Work 6 (4, *6*, 6) rows stocking st.

SHAPE SHOULDER

Cast off 6 (6, 7, 7) sts at beg of next row and foll alt row.

Work 1 row. Cast off.

Join yarn to rem sts and work other side to correspond.

Sleeves

Using 2.00 mm needles, cast on 39 (39, *41*, 41) sts.

1st row K2, ★ P1, K1, rep from ★ to last st, K1.

2nd row K1, ★ P1, K1, rep from ★ to end.

Rep 1st and 2nd rows 3 (3, 4, 4) times, then 1st row once.

Next row Rib 4 (6, 6, 4), ★ inc in next st, rib 5 (2, 1, 1), rep from ★ to last 5 (6, 9, 7) sts, inc in next st, rib to end... 45 (49, 55, 57) sts.

Change to 2.75 mm needles.

Work 4 rows stocking st.

5th row K2, "M1", knit to last 2 sts, "M1", K2.

Cont in stocking st, inc (as before) at each end of foll 4th (6th, *6th*, 8th) rows until there are 51 (59, *65*, 71) sts. **Sizes A, B and C only**, then in foll 6th (8th, *8th*) row/s until there are 55 (61, *69*) sts. **All sizes**, cont without shaping until work measures 13 (16, *19*, 21) cm from beg, ending with a purl row.

Tie a coloured thread at each end of last row to mark end of sleeve seam.

Work a further 6 (6, 8, 10) rows stocking st.

Cast off 4 (5, 5, 6) sts at beg of next 10 rows. Cast off rem sts.

Neckband

Using backstitch, join shoulder seams. With right side facing and using 2.00 mm needles, knit up 78 (78, 86, 86) sts evenly around neck.

Knit 2 rows garter st. Cast off *loosely*.

Make up

With a slightly damp cloth and warm iron, press lightly, taking care not to flatten patt. Using backstitch, join side and sleeve seams to coloured threads. Sew in sleeves, placing rows above coloured threads to sts cast off at armholes. Turn lower edge onto wrong side at row of holes and slipstitch in position. Sew underlap in position. Sew on buttons. Press seams and hem.

Cut 2 collar shapes from fabric. Stitch collars tog with right sides inside, using a 6 mm seam and leaving a 3 cm opening at lower edge. Clip curves, turn collar to right side and slipstitch closed. Attach lace to outside edge of collar, turning raw edges under. Sew button to wrong side of collar and make a buttonloop to correspond.

Note To make shoes in photo see pattern page 29. For fabric trim see *Make up* on page 34.

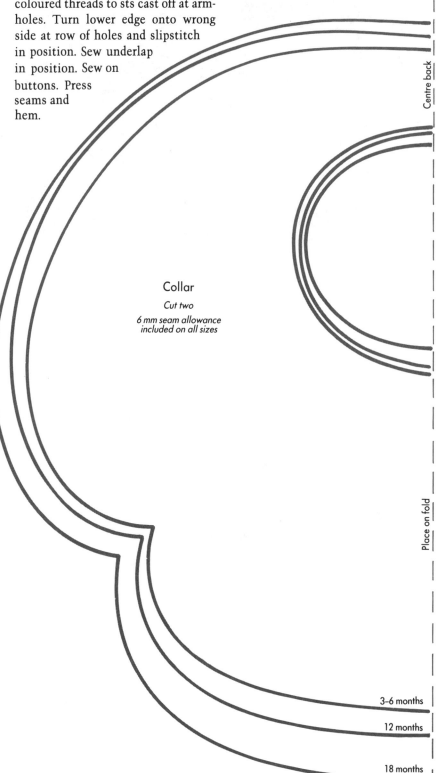

Collar

Cut two

*6 mm seam allowance
included on all sizes*

Centre back

Place on fold

3–6 months

12 months

18 months

Cot Blanket

MEASUREMENTS

Width (approx)	cm	74
	ins	29
Length (approx)	cm	114
	ins	45

MATERIALS

| Patons Totem 8 Ply | 12 |
| 50 g balls | |

ACCESSORIES

1 pair 4.00 mm (no. 8) Milward knitting needles or size needed to give correct tension, 1.5 metres of 90 cm wide Liberty fabric (we used fabric no. 332022.M).

TENSION

22.5 sts to 10 cm in width over stocking st, using 4.00 mm needles.
Please check your tension carefully. If less sts use smaller needles, if more sts use bigger needles.

Cast on 167 sts.
Note If this number of sts will not fit comfortably on needle, we suggest using a circular needle.
Knit 4 rows garter st (1st row is wrong side).
5th row K4, purl to last 4 sts, K4.
6th row Knit.
Rep 5th and 6th rows until work measures 113 cm from beg, ending with a 5th row.
Knit 3 rows garter st. Cast off *loosely*.

Make up

With a slightly damp cloth and warm iron, press lightly. Lay fabric flat with wrong side up. Lay blanket on top (in centre of fabric) with right side up. Turning raw edges under, fold fabric over onto blanket. Pin in place, mitring corners. Handstitch in place, sewing through all layers. Press edges.

Little boy blue

Even a beginner can produce a special occasion outfit by adding fabric trim to this jacket, hat and shoes

MEASUREMENTS

The jacket is designed to be a generous fit.

Size		A	B	C	D
Approx age	months	3	6	12	18
JACKET					
Fits underarm	cm	40	45	50	52.5
	ins	16	18	20	21
Garment measures	cm	45	50	56	58.5
Length	cm	27	30	34	37
Sleeve fits	cm	13	16	19	21
HAT					
Fits head	cm	40	45	48	49.5
SHOES					
Length of foot (approx)	cm	8	9.5	11	12.5

MATERIALS

Patons Gem Cotton 4 Ply 50 g balls

	A	B	C	D
Jacket	2	3	3	4
Hat	1	1	1	1
Shoes	1	1	1	1

ACCESSORIES

1 pair each 2.75 mm (no. 12) and 2.00 mm (no. 14) Milward knitting needles, 2.00 mm (no. 14) circular needle for Jacket, or sizes needed to give correct tension, 2 buttons for Shoes, 2.8 (3, *3.2, 3.4*) metres 2 cm wide Liberty fabric bias trim (we used fabric no. 339010.G) for Jacket and Shoes, 15 cm of 90 cm wide matching Liberty fabric and 7 cm of 90 cm wide fine wadding for Hat.

TENSION

29 sts to 10 cm in width over stocking st, using 2.75 mm needles.
Please check your tension carefully. If less sts use smaller needles, if more sts use bigger needles.

Jacket

Back

Using 2.75 mm needles, cast on 67 (75, *83, 87*) sts.
Work in reverse stocking st until work measures 17 (19, *21,* 23.5) cm from beg, ending with a knit row.
Tie a coloured thread at each end of last row to mark beg of armholes as there is no armhole shaping.
Work a further 38 (40, *48, 50*) rows reverse stocking st.

SHAPE SHOULDERS

Cast off 7 (8, *9, 9*) sts at beg of next 4 rows, then 7 (8, *9, 11*) sts at beg of foll 2 rows.

Cast off rem 25 (27, *29, 29*) sts.

Left Front

Using 2.75 mm needles, cast on 23 (25, *27, 29*) sts.
Work in reverse stocking st, inc at end of first row, then at same edge in every row until there are 29 (31, *33, 35*) sts, in alt rows until there are 30 (35, *38, 40*) sts, then in foll 4th rows until there are 33 (37, *41, 43*) sts.
Tie a coloured thread at beg of last row to mark end of curve.
Cont in reverse stocking st until work measures 17 (19, *21,* 23.5) cm from beg, ending with a knit row.
Tie a coloured thread at end of last row to mark beg of armhole.
Work a further 24 (26, *32, 34*) rows reverse stocking st.

SHAPE NECK

Next row P27 (30, *34, 34*), *turn* and leave rem 6 (7, *7, 9*) sts on a safety pin.
Dec at neck edge in alt rows until 21 (24, *27, 27*) sts rem.
Work 1 row.

SHAPE SHOULDER

Cast off 7 (8, *9, 9*) sts at beg of next row and foll alt row.
Work 1 row. Cast off.

Right Front

Work to correspond with Left Front, reversing shapings.

Sleeves

Using 2.00 mm needles, cast on 43 (45, *49, 53*) sts.

Knit 5 rows garter st (1st row is wrong side).

Change to 2.75 mm needles.

Work in reverse stocking st, inc at each end of 5th and foll 6th (6th, *4th*, 6th) rows until there are 51 (57, *63*, 71) sts. **Size C only**, then in foll 6th rows until there are 69 sts. **All sizes**, cont without shaping until work measures 11 (14, *17*, 19) cm from beg, ending with a knit row.

Cast off 4 (5, *5*, 5) sts at beg of next 8 rows.

Cast off rem sts.

Neckband

Using backstitch, join shoulder seams. With right side facing and using 2.00 mm needles, knit up 67 (71, *77*, 81) sts evenly around neck, incl sts from safety pins.

Knit 4 rows garter st. Cast off.

Edging

Using backstitch, join side seams to coloured threads. With right side facing and using 2.00 mm circular needle, knit up 73 (81, *87*, 99) sts evenly along Left Front edge to coloured thread (incl end of Neckband), 26 (31, *36*, 38) sts around curve to cast-on edge, 109 (121, *133*, 141) sts along cast-on edge of Fronts and Back, 26 (31, *36*, 38) sts around curve to coloured thread, then 73 (81, *87*, 99) sts evenly along Right Front edge to top of Neckband… 307 (345, *379*, 415) sts.

Knit 4 rows garter st. Cast off *loosely*.

Make up

With a slightly damp cloth and warm iron, press lightly. Using backstitch, join sleeve seams. Sew in sleeves. Bind all edges of jacket and sleeves with bias trim, sewing inside edge first, then folding trim and sewing outside edge. Cut two 25 cm lengths for ties and sew folded edges tog. Tie a knot at one end and sew other end to neck edge. Press seams.

Hat

Using 2.00 mm needles, cast on 121 (129, *137*, 145) sts.

1st row K2, ★ P1, K1, rep from ★ to last st, K1.

2nd row K1, ★ P1, K1, rep from ★ to end.

Rep 1st and 2nd rows 3 times … 8 rows rib in all.

Change to 2.75 mm needles.

Work in reverse stocking st until work measures 7 (7.5, *8*, 8.5) cm from beg, working last row on right side.

SHAPE CROWN

1st row K1, ★ K2 tog, K13 (14, *15*, 16), rep from ★ to end.

2nd and 4th rows Purl.

3rd row K1, ★ K2 tog, K12 (13, *14*, 15), rep from ★ to end.

5th row K1, ★ K2 tog, K11 (12, *13*, 14), rep from ★ to end.

Cont in reverse stocking st, dec in this manner (working one st less between dec each time in alt rows) until 17 sts rem.

Break off yarn, run end through rem sts, draw up and fasten off securely.

Make up

With a slightly damp cloth and warm iron, press lightly. Using backstitch, join seam. Press seam. Place hat on child's head and measure circumference of lower edge. Cut fabric and wadding this length plus 4 cm for ease and seam. Join ends of fabric, then fold in half lengthways with wadding inside. Pin raw edges to lower edge of hat, stretching hat evenly to fit, then sew using a large zig-zag stitch.

Shoes

Using 2.75 mm needles, cast on 29 (37, *45*, 53) sts.

1st and alt rows (wrong side) Knit.

2nd row K1, ★ "M1", K13 (17, *21*, 25), "M1", K1, rep from ★ once.

4th row K1, ★ "M1", K15 (19, *23*, 27), "M1", K1, rep from ★ once.

6th row K1, ★ "M1", K17 (21, *25*, 29), "M1", K1, rep from ★ once.

8th row K1, ★ "M1", K19 (23, *27*, 31), "M1", K1, rep from ★ once.

10th row K1, ★ "M1", K21 (25, *29*, 33), "M1", K1, rep from ★ once … 49 (57, *65*, 73) sts.

11th and 12th rows Knit.

13th row K1, purl to last st, K1.

Rep 12th and 13th rows 2 (2, *3*, 3) times.

SHAPE INSTEP

1st row K27 (31, *35*, 39), sl 1, K1, psso, K1, *turn*.

2nd row P7, P2 tog, P1, *turn*.

3rd row K8, sl 1, K1, psso, K1, *turn*.

4th row P9, P2 tog, P1, *turn*.

5th row K10, sl 1, K1, psso, *turn*.

6th row P10, P2 tog, *turn*.

Rep 5th and 6th rows 1 (2, *3*, 4) time/s.

Next row Knit to end … 41 (47, *53*, 59) sts.

Next row Knit.

Next row K14 (17, *20*, 23), K2 tog, K9, sl 1, K1, psso, K14 (17, *20*, 23).

Cast off.

Straps

Using 2.75 mm needles, cast on 33 (36, *39*, 42) sts.

1st row (wrong side) Knit.

2nd row K2, y fwd, K2 tog (buttonhole), knit to end.

Cast off *loosely*.

Make up

With a slightly damp cloth and warm iron, press lightly. Using a flat seam, join back and foot seams. Sew centre of strap to back of shoe for 2 cm each side of seam. (Take care to reverse strap on second shoe so that buttonhole is at other end.) Sew on buttons. Cut a 7 cm length of bias trim for each shoe. Stitch folded edges tog, then take a running thread along this stitched edge. Pull up tightly so that fabric gathers up into a small circle. Stitch the raw edges tog, then sew to front of shoe.

Daffy-Down-Dilly

This reversible jacket made from two identical pieces will keep baby warm on the coldest of days

MEASUREMENTS

This garment is designed to be a generous fit.

Size		A	B	C
Approx age	months	3	6	12
Fits underarm	cm	40	45	50
	ins	16	18	20
Garment measures	*cm*	*45*	*51*	*57*
Length	cm	27	30	34
Sleeve fits	cm	13	16	19

MATERIALS

Patons Bluebell 5 Ply or Patons 5 Ply Machinewash 50 g balls

1st colour (C1)	3	4	5
2nd colour (C2)	3	4	5

ACCESSORIES

1 pair 3.75 mm (no. 9) Milward knitting needles or size needed to give correct tension, length of ribbon.

TENSION

26.5 sts and 35 rows to 10 cm over stocking st.
Please check your tension carefully. If less sts use smaller needles, if more sts use bigger needles.
Note Jacket is completely reversible. Make 2 identical pieces for Jacket and Hood, 1 in C1 and 1 in C2.

Jacket

Worked in one piece, beg at lower edge of Back.
Using 3.75 mm needles and C1, cast on 62 (70, 78) sts *loosely*.
Work in stocking st until work measures 18 (20, 23) cm from beg, ending with a purl row.

SHAPE FOR SLEEVES

Cast on 45 (53, 63) sts at beg of next 2 rows… 152 (176, 204) sts.
Note If this number of sts will not fit comfortably on needle, we suggest using a circular needle.

Work a further 30 (34, 38) rows stocking st.

SHAPE BACK NECK

Next row K64 (75, 88), cast off 24 (26, 28) sts *loosely*, knit to end.
Cont on last 64 (75, 88) sts for **Left Front**.
Work 3 rows stocking st.
Inc at beg (neck edge) of next and alt rows until there are 69 (80, 94) sts.
Work 1 row.
Cast on 7 (8, 8) sts at beg of next row… 76 (88, 102) sts.
Work a further 18 (22, 24) rows stocking st.

SHAPE SLEEVE

Cast off 45 (53, 63) sts at beg of next row… 31 (35, 39) sts.
Cont without shaping until front measures same as back to cast-on edge, ending with a purl row. Cast off *loosely*.
Join yarn to rem sts for **Right Front** and work to correspond with Left Front.

Hood

Using 3.75 mm needles and C1, cast on 114 (126, 140) sts.
Work 54 (54, 56) rows stocking st.

SHAPE BACK

Cast off 6 sts at beg of next 12 (14, 16) rows.
Cast off rem 42 (42, 44) sts.

Make up

With a slightly damp cloth and warm iron, press lightly. Using backstitch, join side, sleeve and hood seams, noting to sew C1 pieces with the stocking st side as the right side and C2 pieces with the purl side as the right side. Place the 2 jackets tog with the right sides inside and sew tog around all edges except neck edge. Turn to right side with C1 side out. Join hood pieces tog in same manner around face edge only and turn to right side. Using a flat seam, sew hood to jacket around neck edge. Press seams. Turn up 3 to 4 cm on sleeves to form cuffs. Sew ribbon in position at neck edge and halfway down front.

Hey diddle diddle

Have lots of fun choosing colour combinations for this woolly jumpsuit, cardigan, jumper, pants, hat and shoes which can be mixed and matched in any way

MEASUREMENTS — JUMPSUIT

This garment is designed to be a generous fit.

Size		A	B	C	D
Approx age	months	3	6	12	18
Fits underarm	cm	40	45	50	52.5
	ins	16	18	20	21
Length	cm	46	53	60	67
Sleeve fits	cm	13	16	19	21

MATERIALS

Patons Bluebell 5 Ply or Patons 5 Ply Machinewash 50 g balls

Main colour (M)	4	5	5	6
1st contrast (C1)	1	1	1	1
2nd contrast (C2)	1	1	1	1
3rd contrast (C3)	1	1	1	1

ACCESSORIES

1 pair each 3.75 mm (no. 9) and 3.00 mm (no. 11) Milward knitting needles or sizes needed to give correct tension, 1 stitch holder, 7 (7, 9, 9) small buttons, 5 large buttons.

TENSION

26.5 sts to 10 cm in width over stocking st, using 3.75 mm needles.
Please check your tension carefully. If less sts use smaller needles, if more sts use bigger needles.

Jumpsuit

Left Leg

Using 3.00 mm needles and C1, cast on 41 (45, 47, 49) sts.

1st row K2, ★ P1, K1, rep from ★ to last st, K1.

2nd row K1, ★ P1, K1, rep from ★ to end.

Rep 1st and 2nd rows 3 (3, 4, 4) times, then 1st row once.

Next row Rib 4, ★ inc in next st, rib 1, rep from ★ to last 1 (5, 3, 5) st/s, rib 1 (5, 3, 5)... 59 (63, 67, 69) sts, 10 (10, 12, 12) rows rib in all.

Change to 3.75 mm needles and M. Work 4 rows stocking st.

5th row K2, "M1", knit to last 2 sts, "M1", K2.

Cont in stocking st, inc (as before) at each end of foll alt (4th, *4th*, 6th) rows until there are 65 (79, 73, 89) sts, then in foll 4th (6th, *6th*, 8th) rows until there are 77 (83, 89, 93) sts.

Work 5 (7, 5, 5) rows stocking st. ★★
Leave rem sts on stitch holder.

Right Leg

Work as for Left Leg to ★★, using C2 instead of C1 for band.
Join legs as foll.

Next row Cast on 3 (3, 4, 4) sts, work across Right Leg sts, *turn*, cast on 4 (4, 6, 6) sts, *turn*, work across Left Leg sts, *turn*, cast on 3 (3, 4, 4) sts... 164 (176, *192*, 200) sts.

Cont in stocking st until work measures 19 (21, 23, 25.5) cm from last cast-on sts, ending with a purl row.

Next row K1 (3, 7, 0), ★ K2 tog, K1 (2, 2, 3), K2 tog, K2, rep from ★ to last 2 (5, 9, 2) sts, K2 tog, K0 (3, 7, 0)... 117 (133, *147*, 155) sts.

Next row Purl.

DIVIDE FOR FRONTS AND BACK

Next row K29 (33, 37, 39), *turn* and cont on these sts for **Right Front**.
Work 25 (27, *29*, 31) rows stocking st.

SHAPE NECK

Cast off 4 sts at beg of next row.
Work 1 row.
Dec at neck edge in every row until 22 (26, 28, 30) sts rem, then in alt rows until 19 (23, 25, 27) sts rem.

SHAPE SHOULDER

Cast off 5 (6, 6, 7) sts at beg of next and alt rows 3 times in all.
Work 1 row. Cast off.
Join yarn to rem sts, K59 (67, 73, 77), *turn* and cont on these sts for **Back**.
Work 35 (37, *41*, 43) rows stocking st.

SHAPE SHOULDERS

Cast off 5 (6, 6, 7) sts at beg of next 6 rows, then 4 (5, 7, 6) sts at beg of foll 2 rows.
Leave rem 21 (21, 23, 23) sts on stitch holder.
Join yarn to rem 29 (33, 37, 39) sts for **Left Front** and work to correspond with Right Front.

Sleeves

Using 3.00 mm needles and *C1 for Right Sleeve* or *C2 for Left Sleeve*, cast on 33 (35, 37, 39) sts.

Work 10 (10, *12*, 12) rows rib as for Left Leg, inc 6 (8, 8, 8) sts evenly across last row... 39 (43, *45*, 47) sts.

Change to 3.75 mm needles and M. Work 4 rows stocking st.

5th row K2, "M1", knit to last 2 sts, "M1", K2.

Cont in stocking st, inc (as before) at each end of foll 4th (6th, *6th*, 6th) rows until there are 53 (57, *61*, 65) sts. Cont without shaping until work measures 13 (16, *19*, 21) cm from beg, ending with a purl row. Cast off 7 sts at beg of next 6 rows. Cast off rem sts.

Front Leg Band

Using backstitch, join centre front seam for 4 cm.

With right side facing, using 3.00 mm needles and M, knit up 41 (56, *61*, 73) sts evenly along front edge of Right Leg, then 41 (56, *61*, 73) sts evenly along front edge of Left Leg... 82 (112, *122*, 146) sts.

Knit 1 row garter st.

2nd row K4, ★ cast off 2 sts, K10 (15, *12*, 15), rep from ★ to last 6 sts, cast off 2 sts, K4.

3rd row K4, ★ *turn*, cast on 2 sts, *turn*, K10 (15, *12*, 15), rep from ★ to last 4 sts, *turn*, cast on 2 sts, *turn*, K4... 7 (7, *9*, 9) buttonholes.

Knit 3 rows garter st. Cast off *loosely*.

Back Leg Band

Work as for Front Leg Band, omitting buttonholes.

Neckband

Using backstitch, join shoulder seams. With right side facing, using 3.00 mm needles and C3, knit up 63 (63, *69*, 69) sts evenly around neck, incl sts from stitch holder.

Work 7 rows rib as for Back. Cast off *loosely* in rib.

Right Front Band

With right side facing, using 3.00 mm needles and M, knit up 59 (63, *67*, 71) sts evenly along Right Front edge, incl end of Neckband.

Knit 1 row.

2nd row K4, ★ cast off 3 sts, K9 (10, *11*, 12), rep from ★ to last 7 sts, cast off 3 sts, K4.

3rd row K4, ★ *turn*, cast on 3 sts, *turn*, K9 (10, *11*, 12), rep from ★ to last 4 sts, *turn*, cast on 3 sts, *turn*, K4... 5 buttonholes.

Knit 3 rows garter st. Cast off *loosely*.

Left Front Band

Work as for Right Front Band, omitting buttonholes.

Make up

With a slightly damp cloth and warm iron, press lightly. Using backstitch, join sleeve seams. Sew in sleeves. Sew buttons in position. Using Knitting Stitch (see page 40), embroider spots from graph (see page 44) in contrast colours at random as illustrated. Press seams.

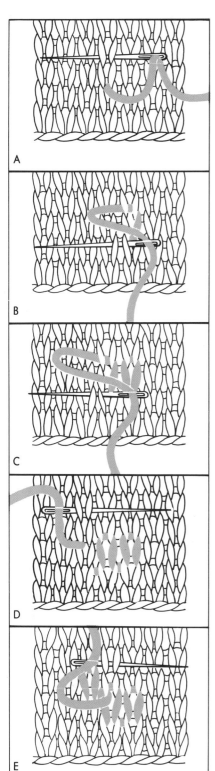

KNITTING STITCH EMBROIDERY

Interest can be added to garments with Knitting Stitch embroidery — this is very easy to do, especially if you do the embroidery before you sew up the garment. Knitting Stitch is worked over each knitted stitch with a contrasting colour. It is necessary to use yarn of the same thickness as the knitted garment. Be careful not to pull the stitch too tightly and it will cover the existing stitch completely.

A completed stitch looks like a "V". Each square on the graph represents one stitch.

Begin at lower edge of graph, on the right-hand side.

Using a tapestry or knitter's needle, bring the needle from the back through the centre of the stitch below the one to be covered (A).

★ Take needle from right to left under both strands of stitch above the one to be covered (B).

Bring needle back to the start of the stitch, take needle behind 2 strands in row below and across into the centre of next stitch. You have worked one Knitting Stitch (C).

Repeat from ★ following graph for required number of stitches. To finish, bring needle back to the start of the stitch and through to the back of the work.

To begin the second row, bring needle from back to centre of stitch below the one to be covered. Working from left to right pick up both strands of stitch in row above the one to be covered (D).

Take needle back to beginning of stitch, pick up 2 strands, which brings the needle across into centre of next stitch (E). When working stitch above one worked in the previous row your needle will come up in the centre of this worked stitch. Repeat this, following graph for number of stitches to be worked.

MEASUREMENTS — RAGLAN SLEEVED JACKET
This garment is designed to be a generous fit.

Size		A	B	C	D
Approx age	months	3	6	12	18
Fits underarm	cm	40	45	50	52.5
	ins	16	18	20	21
Garment measures	cm	46	51.5	56.5	59.5
Length	cm	24	27	31	33.5
Sleeve fits	cm	13	16	19	21

MATERIALS
Patons Bluebell 5 Ply 50 g balls	2	3	3	4

ACCESSORIES

1 pair each 3.75 mm (no. 9) and 3.00 mm (no. 11) Milward knitting needles or sizes needed to give correct tension, 1 stitch holder, 5 buttons.

TENSION

26.5 sts to 10 cm in width over stocking st, using 3.75 mm needles.
Please check your tension carefully. If less sts use smaller needles, if more sts use bigger needles.

Jacket

Back

Using 3.75 mm needles, cast on 63 (69, 77, 81) sts.

1st row
K2, ★ P1, K1, rep from ★ to last st, K1.
2nd row K1, ★ P1, K1, rep from ★ to end.
Rep 1st and 2nd rows once… 4 rows rib in all.
Work in stocking st until work measures 12 (14, 17, 19) cm from beg, ending with a purl row.

SHAPE RAGLAN ARMHOLES

Cast off 3 sts at beg of next 2 rows.
Dec at each end of next and foll 4th (4th, *alt*, every) row/s until 53 (59, 23, 69) sts rem. **Sizes A, B and D only**, then in alt rows until 19 (21, 23) sts rem. **All sizes**, work 1 row.
Leave rem sts on stitch holder.

Left Front

Using 3.75 mm needles, cast on 31 (35, 39, 41) sts.
Work 4 rows rib as for Back.
Work in stocking st until work measures same as Back to armholes, ending with a purl row.

SHAPE RAGLAN ARMHOLE

Cast off 3 sts at beg of next row.
Work 1 row.
Dec at armhole edge in next and foll 4th (4th, *alt*, every) row/s until 26 (30, 19, 35) sts rem. **Sizes A, B and D only**, then in alt rows until 15 (17, 19) sts rem.

SHAPE NECK

All sizes Cast off 3 (4, 4, 4) sts at beg of next row.
Dec at each end of next and alt rows until 4 (3, 3, 3) sts rem, then at armhole edge only in alt row/s until 2 sts rem.
Next row P2, *turn*, K2 tog.
Fasten off.

Right Front

Work to correspond with Left Front.

Sleeves

Using 3.75 mm needles, cast on 37 (39, 43, 45) sts.
Work 4 rows rib as for Back.
Work 4 rows stocking st.

5th row K2, "M1", knit to last 2 sts, "M1", K2.
Cont in stocking st, inc (as before) at each end of foll 8th (10th, *12th*, 12th) rows until there are 47 (49, 53, 57) sts.
Cont without shaping until work measures 13 (16, *19*, 21) cm from beg, ending with a purl row.

SHAPE RAGLAN

Cast off 3 sts at beg of next 2 rows.
Dec at each end of next and foll 4th rows until 33 (33, 37, 43) sts rem, then in alt rows until 7 sts rem.
Work 1 row. Cast off.

Left Front Band

Using 3.00 mm needles, cast on 9 sts. Work 74 (82, *98*, 106) rows rib as for Back.
Leave sts on a safety pin, break off yarn.

Right Front Band

Using 3.00 mm needles, cast on 9 sts.
Work 4 rows rib as for Back.
5th row Rib 4, y fwd, K2 tog, rib 3 (buttonhole).
Work 17 (19, 23, 25) rows rib.
Rep last 18 (20, 24, 26) rows twice, then 5th row once… 4 buttonholes. Work 16 (18, 22, 24) rows rib. Do not break off yarn, leave sts on needle.

Neckband

Using backstitch, join raglan seams, noting that tops of Sleeves form part of neckline. Sew Front Bands in position. With right side facing and using 3.00 mm needle holding Right Front Band sts, knit up 49 (53, *59*, 59) sts evenly around neck, incl sts from stitch holder, then rib across Left Front Band sts… 67 (71, 77, 77) sts.
Work 5 rows rib as for Back, beg with a 2nd row and working a buttonhole (as before) in 2nd row… 5 buttonholes.
Cast off *loosely* in rib.

Make up

With a slightly damp cloth and warm iron, press lightly. Using backstitch, join sleeve and side seams. Sew on buttons. Press seams.

MEASUREMENTS — JUMPER, PANTS, HAT AND SHOES

The jumper is designed to be a generous fit.

Size		A	B	C	D
Approx age	months	3	6	12	18

JUMPER

Fits underarm	cm	40	45	50	52.5
	ins	16	18	20	21
Garment measures	cm	44	49.5	55	58
Length	cm	23	26	29	32
Sleeve fits	cm	13	16	19	21

PANTS

Length to ankle (approx)	cm	27	32	37	42

HAT

Fits head	cm	40	45	48	49.5

SHOES

Fit foot (approx)	cm	8	9.5	11	12.5

MATERIALS

Patons Bluebell 5 Ply *or* Patons 5 Ply Machinewash 50 g balls

JUMPER

1st colour (C1)	2	3	3	4
2nd colour (C2)	1	1	1	1
3rd colour (C3)	1	1	1	1
4th colour (C4)	1	1	1	1

PANTS

3rd colour (C3)	3	3	3	4
4th colour (C4)	1	1	1	1

HAT

1st colour (C1)	1	1	1	1
2nd colour (C2)	small quantity for each size			

SHOES

1st colour (C1)	1	1	1	1
2nd colour (C2)	small quantity for each size			

ACCESSORIES

1 pair each 3.75 mm (no. 9) and 3.00 mm (no. 11) Milward knitting needles or sizes needed to give correct tension, 3 stitch holders and 4 buttons for Jumper, length of round elastic for Pants, padding for Hat, 2 buttons for Shoes.

TENSION

25 sts and 52 rows to 10 cm over garter st, using 3.75 mm needles.
Please check your tension carefully. If less sts use smaller needles, if more sts use bigger needles.

Jumper

Back

Using 3.00 mm needles and C2, cast on 57 (63, 69, 75) sts.
1st row K2, ★ P1, K1, rep from ★ to last st, K1.

2nd row K1, ★ P1, K1, rep from ★ to end.
Rep 1st and 2nd rows 5 times... 12 rows rib in all.
Change to 3.75 mm needles and C1.

Knit in garter st until work measures 12 (14, *16*, 18.5) cm from beg, working last row on wrong side.

SHAPE RAGLAN

Cast off 2 sts at beg of next 2 rows.
Knit 2 rows garter st. ★★
Dec at each end of next and foll 4th rows until 43 (47, 49, 53) sts rem.
Knit 1 row.

DIVIDE FOR BACK OPENING

1st row K24 (26, 27, 29), *turn*, and cont on these sts.
2nd row Knit.
3rd row K2 tog, knit to end.
4th, 5th and 6th rows Knit.
7th row K2 tog, knit to last 3 sts, y fwd, K2 tog (buttonhole), K1.
8th, 9th and 10th rows As 2nd row.
Rep rows 3 to 6 incl twice, then 7th row once.
Dec at armhole edge in foll 4th (4th, *4th*, alt) rows until 15 (18, *20*, 17) sts rem. **Sizes B and C only**, then in alt rows until (16, *17*) sts rem. **All sizes, at same time** working a buttonhole (as before) in foll 12th row from previous buttonhole... 3 buttonholes in all.
Knit 1 row. Leave sts on a stitch holder.
Join yarn to rem sts, cast on 5 sts for underlap and work to correspond with other side, omitting buttonholes.

Front

Work as for Back to ★★.
Dec at each end of next and foll 4th rows until 37 (41, 47, 51) sts rem.
Knit 1 row.

SHAPE NECK

Next row K14 (15, 17, 19), *turn* and cont on these sts.
Knit 1 row.
Dec at armhole edge in next and foll 4th rows 6 (5, 6, 4) times in all, then in alt rows 0 (2, 3, 7) times, **at same time** dec at neck edge in alt rows 5 (5, 3, 3) times, then in foll 4th row/s 1 (1, 3, 3) time/s... 2 sts.
Next row K2, *turn*, K2 tog. Fasten off.
Slip next 9 (11, *13*, 13) sts onto a stitch

holder and leave. Join yarn to rem sts and work other side to correspond.

Sleeves

Using 3.00 mm needles and C4, cast on 33 (35, 37, 37) sts.
Work 12 rows rib as for Back, inc 4 sts evenly across last row... 37 (39, 41, 41) sts.
Change to 3.75 mm needles and C1.
Knit in garter st, inc at each end of 5th and foll 14th (14th, 16th, 16th) rows until there are 43 (47, 49, 51) sts.
Cont in garter st until work measures 13 (16, 19, 21) cm from beg, working last row on wrong side.

SHAPE RAGLAN
Cast off 2 sts at beg of next 2 rows.
Dec at each end of next and foll 4th rows until 11 (13, 11, 11) sts rem. **Sizes A and B only**, then in alt rows until 9 (11) sts rem. **All sizes**, knit 1 row.
Cast off.

Neckband

Using backstitch, join raglan seams, noting that tops of Sleeves form part of neckline. With right side facing, using 3.00 mm needles and C3, knit up 83 (91, 107, 107) sts evenly around neck, incl sts from stitch holders.
1st row (wrong side) K5, ★ P1, K1, rep from ★ to last 4 sts, K4.
2nd row K6, ★ P1, K1, rep from ★ to last 5 sts, K5.
Rep 1st and 2nd rows 3 times, then 1st row once, working a buttonhole (as before) in 12th row from previous buttonhole. Cast off in rib.

Make up

We do not recommend pressing this garment, owing to the texture. Using backstitch, join side and sleeve seams. Sew underlap in position. Sew on buttons. Press seams.

Pants

Left Leg

Using 3.00 mm needles and C4, cast on 41 (45, 47, 49) sts.
Work 11 rows rib as for Back of Jumper.
12th row Rib 3 (5, 5, 5), inc in each st to last 4 (6, 4, 6) sts, rib 4 (6, 4, 6)... 75 (79, 85, 87) sts.
Change to 3.75 mm needles and C3.
Knit in garter st until work measures 11 (15, 19, 23) cm from beg, working last row on wrong side.

SHAPE CROTCH
Cast on 2 (2, 2, 3) sts at beg of next 2 rows... 79 (83, 89, 93) sts.
Cont in garter st until work measures 15 (16, 17, 18) cm from beg of crotch, working last row on wrong side. ★★

SHAPE BACK
Note When turning, bring yarn to front of work, slip next st onto right-hand needle, y bk, slip st back onto left-hand needle, then turn and proceed as instructed — this avoids holes in work.

1st row K60 (60, 65, 65), *turn.*
2nd and alt rows Knit to end.
3rd row K55 (55, 60, 60), *turn.*
5th row K50 (50, 55, 55), *turn.*
Cont in this manner, working 5 sts less in alt rows until the row "K25 (25, 30, 30), *turn*" has been worked.
Next row As 2nd row. ★★★
Change to 3.00 mm needles and C4.
Knit 1 row, then work 11 rows rib as before, beg with a 2nd row.
Cast off *loosely* in rib.

Right Leg

Work as for Left Leg to ★★ working 1 row less.

Shape Back as for Left Leg to ★★★. Knit 1 row.

Change to 3.00 mm needles and C4.
Knit 1 row, then work 11 rows rib as before, beg with a 2nd row.
Cast off *loosely* in rib.

Make up

We do not recommend pressing this garment, owing to the texture. Using backstitch, join front, back and leg seams. Thread round elastic through 1st, 5th and 9th rows of rib at waistband and draw up to desired measurement.

Cont dec in this manner (working one st less between dec each time), in alt rows until 13 sts rem.
Break off yarn, run end through rem sts, draw up and fasten off securely.

Make up

We do not recommend pressing this garment, owing to the texture. Using backstitch, join back seam, reversing seam for rib. Turn back band, then pad and slipstitch in position.

Shoes

Using 3.75 mm needles and C2, cast on 31 (37, *43*, 49) sts.
1st and alt rows (wrong side) Knit.
2nd row   [K1, "M1", K14 (17, *20*, 23), "M1"] twice, K1.

Hat

Using 3.00 mm needles and C2, cast on 107 (119, *127*, 131) sts.
Work 22 rows rib as for Back of Jumper, dec 4 (10, *6*, 4) sts evenly across last row... 103 (109, *121*, 127) sts.
Change to 3.75 mm needles and C1.
Knit in garter st until work measures 10 (11, *12*, 13) cm from centre row of rib, working last row on wrong side.

SHAPE CROWN

1st row   K1, ★ K2 tog, K15 (16, *18*, 19), rep from ★ to end.
2nd and alt rows   Knit.
3rd row   K1, ★ K2 tog, K14 (15, *17*, 18), rep from ★ to end.
5th row   K1, ★ K2 tog, K13 (14, *16*, 17), rep from ★ to end.

4th row   [K1, "M1", K16 (19, *22*, 25), "M1"] twice, K1.
6th row   [K1, "M1", K18 (21, *24*, 27), "M1"] twice, K1.
8th row   [K1, "M1", K20 (23, *26*, 29), "M1"] twice, K1... 47 (53, *59*, 65) sts.
Knit 13 (15, *17*, 19) rows.

SHAPE INSTEP

1st row   K28 (31, *34*, 37), sl 1 knitways, K1, psso, *turn*.
2nd row   K10, sl 1 knitways, K1, psso, *turn*.
Rep 2nd row 4 times.
Using C1 for rem, **7th row**   As 2nd row.

8th row   (P1 K1) 5 times, P2 tog, *turn*.
9th row   (K1, P1) 5 times, y bk, sl 1 knitways, K1, psso, *turn*.
Rep 8th and 9th rows 2 (3, *4*, 5) times, then 8th row once.
Next row   (K1, P1) 5 times, knit to end... 33 (37, *41*, 45) sts.
Next row   (K1, P1) 11 (12, *13*, 14) times, purl to end.
Next row   K2, ★ P1, K1, rep from ★ to last st, K1.
Next row   K1, ★ P1, K1, rep from ★ to end.
Rep last 2 rows 9 (10, *11*, 12) times.
Cast off *loosely* in rib.

Straps

Using 3.75 mm needles and C2, cast on 15 sts.
1st row (wrong side)   Knit.
2nd row   K12, y fwd, K2 tog (buttonhole), K1. Cast off *loosely*.

Make up

Do not press. Using a flat seam, join leg and foot seams. Sew strap in position and sew on button to correspond with buttonhole. Take care to sew button on opposite side on second shoe.

Key for Knitting Stitch embroidery
☐ Main colour
☑ Contrast

Monday's child

A perky little eyelet striped jacket and hat to provide that little extra warmth on cooler days

MEASUREMENTS

The jacket is designed to be a generous fit.

Size		A	B	C	D
Approx age	months	0	3	6	12
JACKET					
Fits underarm	cm	35	40	45	50
	ins	14	16	18	20
Garment measures	*cm*	38	43.5	49	54.5
Length	cm	21	24	27	31
Sleeve fits	cm	11	13	16	19
HAT					
Fits head	cm	35	40	45	48

MATERIALS

Patons Feathersoft 4 Ply 25 g balls

JACKET				
Main colour (M)	2	2	3	3
1st contrast (C1)	1	1	1	1
2nd contrast (C2)	1	1	1	1
HAT				
Main colour (M)	1	1	1	1
1st and 2nd contrasts	small quantity for each size			

ACCESSORIES

1 pair each 3.25 mm (no. 10) and 2.75 mm (no. 12) Milward knitting needles or sizes needed to give correct tension.

TENSION

29 sts to 10 cm in width over stocking st, using 3.25 mm needles.
Please check your tension carefully. If less sts use smaller needles, if more sts use bigger needles.

Jacket

Back

Using 2.75 mm needles and C1, cast on 57 (65, 73, 81) sts.
1st row K2, ★ P1, K1, rep from ★ to last st, K1.
2nd row K1, ★ P1, K1, rep from ★ to end.
Rep 1st and 2nd rows 5 (5, 6, 6) times... 12 (12, 14, 14) rows rib in all.
Change to 3.25 mm needles and M.
Work 12 rows stocking st.
13th and 14th rows Using C2, knit.
15th row Using C2, K1, ★ y fwd,

K2 tog, rep from ★ to end.
16th row Using C2, knit.
Using M, work 12 rows stocking st.
29th and 30th rows Using C1, knit.
31st row Using C1, ★ sl 1, K1, psso, y fwd, rep from ★ to last st, K1.
32nd row Using C1, knit.
Last 32 rows form patt.
Cont in patt until work measures 12 (14, 16, 19) cm from beg, working last row on wrong side.

SHAPE ARMHOLES

Keeping patt correct, cast off 2 (3, 3, 4) sts at beg of next 2 rows.
Dec at each end of next and alt rows until 49 (55, 61, 65) sts rem.
Work a further 33 (37, 39, 41) rows patt.

SHAPE SHOULDERS

Keeping patt correct, cast off 5 (5, 6, 7) sts at beg of next 4 rows, then 4 (6, 7, 6) sts at beg of foll 2 rows.
Cast off rem 21 (23, 23, 25) sts.

Left Front

Using 2.75 mm needles and C1, cast on 29 (33, 37, 41) sts.
Work 12 (12, 14, 14) rows rib as for Back.
Change to 3.25 mm needles.
Work in patt as for Back until work measures same as Back to armholes, ending with same row.

SHAPE ARMHOLE AND FRONT SLOPE

Keeping patt correct, cast off 2 (3, 3, 4) sts at beg of next row. Work 1 row.
Dec at each end of next and alt rows until 23 (26, 28, 29) sts rem, then at front edge only in alt rows until 20 (23, 27, 28) sts rem.
Dec at front edge only in foll 4th rows until 14 (16, 19, 20) sts rem.
Work 3 (3, 5, 7) rows patt.

SHAPE SHOULDER

Keeping patt correct, cast off 5 (5, 6, 7) sts at beg of next row and foll alt row. Work 1 row. Cast off.

Right Front

Work to correspond with Left Front.

46

Sleeves

Using 2.75 mm needles and C1, cast on 35 (37, *39*, 41) sts.

Work 12 (12, *14*, 14) rows rib as for Back, inc 4 (4, *4*, 6) sts evenly across last row... 39 (41, *43*, 47) sts.

Change to 3.25 mm needles and M. Working in patt as for Back and working extra sts into patt, inc at each end of 5th and foll 6th (8th, *10th*, 12th) rows until there are 49 (51, *53*, 57) sts. Cont without shaping until work measures 11 (13, *16*, 19) cm from beg, working last row on wrong side.

SHAPE TOP

Keeping patt correct, cast off 2 sts at beg of next 2 rows. Dec at each end of next and alt rows until 25 (21, *21*, 21) sts rem, then in every row until 15 sts rem. Cast off.

Front Band

Using backstitch, join shoulder seams. Using 2.75 mm needles and C1, cast on 9 sts.

Work rib as for Back until band is length required to fit (slightly stretched) along Fronts and across Back neck. Cast off in rib.

Make up

Do not press. Using backstitch, join side and sleeve seams. Sew in sleeves. Sew front band in position.

Hat

Using 2.75 mm needles and C1, cast on 103 (117, *133*, 141) sts.

Work 12 rows rib as for Back of Jacket. Change to 3.25 mm needles.

Work in patt as for Back of Jacket until work measures 12 (13, *14*, 15) cm from beg, working last row on wrong side.

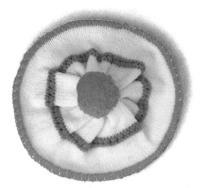

Next row K1, ★ K2 tog, rep from ★ to end... 52 (59, *67*, 71) sts.
Next row Purl.
Next row K0 (1, *1*, 1), ★ K2 tog, rep from ★ to end... 26 (30, *34*, 36) sts.

Break off yarn, run end through rem sts, draw up and fasten off securely.

Make up

Do not press. Using backstitch, join seam. Using C2, make a small pompom and sew on top of hat.

To make a pompom, cut two circles of cardboard, the diameters of which depend on the size of the pompom to be made, and should be equal to the size of the finished pompom plus approximately 1.25 cm for trimming, plus the diameter of the centre hole, e.g. for a pompom 4 cm across, the circles would be 4 cm, plus 1.25 cm, plus 1.25 cm for centre hole, equals 6.5 cm. Cut a round hole in the centre, the size of the hole is approximately a quarter of the finished pompom.

Wind the yarn round and round the cardboard until the centre hole is completely filled up.

Place the point of a pair of scissors between the two circles of cardboard and cut around, keeping the scissors between the cardboard all the time. Using a double strand of yarn, wrap round between the two circles of cardboard, knot firmly, and take away cardboard. Trim pompom.

Tommy Snooks and Bessy Brooks

These smart little tops knitted in an interesting textured pattern are perfect for any occasion

MEASUREMENTS
This garment is designed to be a generous fit.

Size		A	B	C	D
Approx age	months	12	18	24	36
Fits underarm	cm	50	52.5	55	57.5
	ins	20	21	22	23
Garment measures	*cm*	*57*	*60*	*63*	*66*
Length	cm	28	31	33	35
Sleeve fits	cm	19	21	23	25
(or length desired)					

MATERIALS

Patons Stonewash Cotton 8 Ply 50 g balls	4	4	5	5

ACCESSORIES
1 pair each 4.00 mm (no. 8) and 3.00 mm (no. 11) Milward knitting needles or sizes needed to give correct tension, 2 stitch holders, 5 buttons for Cardigan.

TENSION
23.5 sts to 10 cm in width over patt, using 4.00 mm needles.
Please check your tension carefully. If less sts use smaller needles, if more sts use bigger needles.

Jumper

Back

Using 3.00 mm needles, cast on 70 (74, 78, 82) sts.
1st row K2, ★ P2, K2, rep from ★ to end.
2nd row P2, ★ K2, P2, rep from ★ to end.
Rep 1st and 2nd rows 4 times, dec 2 sts evenly across last row... 68 (72, 76, 80) sts, 10 rows rib in all.
Change to 4.00 mm needles.
1st row Knit.
2nd, 4th and 6th rows (K1, P1) 2 (3, 4, 5) times, K1, ★ P2, (K1, P1) twice, K1, rep from ★ to last 0 (2, 4, 6) sts, (P1, K1) 0 (1, 2, 3) time/s.
3rd, 5th and 7th rows (K1, P1) 2 (3, 4, 5) times, ★ K4, P1, K1, P1, rep from ★ to last 1 (3, 5, 7) st/s, K1, (P1, K1) 0 (1, 2, 3) time/s.
8th row K5 (7, 9, 11), ★ P2, K12, rep from ★ to last 7 (9, 11, 13) sts, P2, K5 (7, 9, 11).
9th row P5 (7, 9, 11), ★ K2, P12, rep from ★ to last 7 (9, 11, 13) sts, K2, P5 (7, 9, 11).
10th row Purl.
11th, 13th and 15th rows (P1, K1) 2 (3, 4, 5) times, P1, ★ K2, (P1, K1) twice, P1, rep from ★ to last 0 (2, 4, 6) sts, (K1, P1) 0 (1, 2, 3) time/s.
12th, 14th and 16th rows (P1, K1) 2 (3, 4, 5) times, ★ P4, K1, P1, K1, rep from ★ to last 1 (3, 5, 7) st/s, P1, (K1, P1) 0 (1, 2, 3) time/s.
17th row P12 (14, 16, 18), ★ K2, P12, rep from ★ to last 0 (2, 4, 6) sts, P0 (2, 4, 6).
18th row K12 (14, 16, 18), ★ P2, K12, rep from ★ to last 0 (2, 4, 6) sts, K0 (2, 4, 6).
Last 18 rows form patt.
Cont in patt until work measures 15 (17.5, 19, 20.5) cm from beg, working last row on wrong side.
Tie a coloured thread at each end of last row to mark beg of armholes as there is no armhole shaping. ★★
Work a further 40 (42, 44, 46) rows patt.

SHAPE SHOULDERS
Keeping patt correct, cast off 6 (7, 7, 7) sts at beg of next 6 rows, then 6 (5, 6, 8) sts at beg of foll 2 rows.
Leave rem 20 (20, 22, 22) sts on a stitch holder.

Front

Work as for Back to ★★.
Work a further 22 (24, 24, 26) rows patt.

SHAPE NECK
Next row Patt 30 (32, 34, 36), *turn* and cont on these sts.
Keeping patt correct, dec at neck edge in alt rows until 24 (26, 27, 29) sts rem.
Work 5 rows patt.

SHAPE SHOULDER
Cast off 6 (7, 7, 7) sts at beg of next and alt rows 3 times in all.
Work 1 row. Cast off.
Slip next 8 sts onto stitch holder and leave. Join yarn to rem sts and work other side to correspond.

Sleeves

Using 3.00 mm needles, cast on 34 (34, 38, 38) sts.
Work 10 rows rib as for Back, inc 8 sts evenly across last row... 42 (42, 46, 46) sts.

Change to 4.00 mm needles.

1st row Knit.

2nd row K0 (0, *1*, 1), P1 (1, *2*, 2), ★ (K1, P1) twice, K1, P2, rep from ★ to last 6 (6, *8*, 8) sts, (K1, P1) 3 times, P0 (0, *1*, 1), K0 (0, *1*, 1).

3rd row K2 (2, *4*, 4), ★ P1, K1, P1, K4, rep from ★ to last 5 (5, *7*, 7) sts, P1, K1, P1, K2 (2, *4*, 4).

4th row As 2nd row.

Keeping patt correct as for Back, *as placed* in last 4 rows, and working extra sts into patt, inc at each end of next and foll 6th (6th, *8th*, 8th) rows until there are 56 (58, *60*, 62) sts.

Cont without shaping until work measures 17 (19, *21*, 23) cm (or 2 cm less than length desired to allow for loose fit) from beg, working last row on wrong side.

Cast off 7 (8, 8, 8) sts at beg of next 6 rows. Cast off rem sts.

Neckband

Using backstitch, join right shoulder seam. With right side facing and using 3.00 mm needles, knit up 70 (70, *74*, 74) sts evenly around neck, incl sts from stitch holders and dec 2 sts evenly across back stitch holder.

Work 15 rows rib as for Back.

Cast off *loosely* in rib.

Make up

With a slightly damp cloth and warm iron, press lightly, taking care not to flatten patt. Using backstitch, join left shoulder seam. Join sleeve and side seams to coloured threads. Sew in sleeves. Fold neckband in half onto wrong side and slipstitch in position. Press seams.

Cardigan

Back and Sleeves

Work as for Jumper.

Left Front

Using 3.00 mm needles, cast on 34 (34, *38*, 38) sts.

Work 10 rows rib as for Back, inc 0 (2, *0*, 2) sts evenly across last row... 34 (36, *38*, 40) sts.

Change to 4.00 mm needles.

1st row Knit.

2nd, 4th and 6th rows P1, ★ (K1, P1) twice, K1, P2, rep from ★ to last 5 (7, 9, 11) sts, K1, (P1, K1) 2 (3, 4, 5) times.

3rd, 5th and 7th rows (K1, P1) 2 (3, 4, 5) times, ★ K4, P1, K1, P1, rep from ★ to last 2 sts, K2.

Cont in patt as for Back, *as placed* in last 7 rows, until work measures same as Back to coloured threads, ending with same row.

Tie a coloured thread at end of last row to mark beg of armhole.

Work a further 29 (31, 31, 33) rows patt.

SHAPE NECK

Keeping patt correct, cast off 5 sts at beg of next row.

Dec at neck edge in next and alt rows until 24 (26, 27, 29) sts rem.

Work 1 row patt.

SHAPE SHOULDER

Cast off 6 (7, 7, 7) sts at beg of next and alt rows 3 times in all.

Work 1 row. Cast off.

Right Front

Work to correspond with Left Front.

Neckband

Using backstitch, join shoulder seams. With right side facing and using 3.00 mm needles, knit up 58 (58, 66, 66) sts evenly around neck, dec 2 sts evenly across back stitch holder.

Work 15 rows rib as for Back, beg with a 2nd row.

Cast off *loosely* in rib.

Left Front Band for boy or Right Front Band for girl

Using 3.00 mm needles, cast on 62 (70, 74, 78) sts.

Work 4 rows rib as for Back.

5th row Rib 4, ★ cast off 2 sts, rib 11 (13, 14, 15), rep from ★ 3 times, cast off 2 sts, rib 4.

6th row Rib 4, ★ *turn*, cast on 2 sts, *turn*, rib 11 (13, 14, 15), rep from ★ 3 times, *turn*, cast on 2 sts, *turn*,

Continued on page 109

Bonny Bobby Shafto

Stripes and straps in Stonewash Cotton for the sailor boy or girl in your life

MEASUREMENTS

The jumper is designed to be a generous fit.

Size		A	B	C
Approx age	months	6	12	18

JUMPER

		A	B	C
Fits underarm	cm	45	50	52.5
	ins	18	20	21
Garment measures	*cm*	*47*	*51*	*55*
Length	cm	26	29	32
Sleeve fits	cm	8	8	9

SHORTS

		A	B	C
Outside leg length	cm	28	30	32

MATERIALS

Patons Stonewash Cotton 8 Ply 50 g balls

JUMPER

		A	B	C
Main colour (M)		2	3	3
Contrast (C)		1	1	1

SHORTS

		A	B	C
Main colour (M)		2	2	3
Contrast (C)		2	2	3

ACCESSORIES

1 pair each 4.00 mm (no. 8) and 3.00 mm (no. 11) Milward knitting needles or sizes needed to give correct tension, knitting-in elastic, 3 stitch holders and 3 buttons for Jumper, 2 buttons and length of round elastic for Shorts.

TENSION

22 sts to 10 cm in width over stocking st, using 4.00 mm needles.
Please check your tension carefully. If less sts use smaller needles, if more sts use bigger needles.

Jumper

Back

Using 3.00 mm needles, C and knitting-in elastic tog, cast on 55 (*61, 65*) sts.
1st row K2, ★ P1, K1, rep from ★ to last st, K1.
2nd row K1, ★ P1, K1, rep from ★ to end.

Rep 1st and 2nd rows 4 times, in stripes of 6 rows M, then 2 rows C... 10 rows rib in all.
Change to 4.00 mm needles and M only.
Work in stocking st until work measures 14 (*16, 18.5*) cm from beg, ending with a purl row.
Tie a coloured thread at each end of last row to mark beg of armholes as there is no armhole shaping. ★★
Work a further 12 (*14, 16*) rows stocking st.

DIVIDE FOR BACK OPENING

1st row K30 (*33, 35*), *turn* and cont on these sts.
2nd row K5, purl to end.
3rd row Knit.
Rep 2nd and 3rd rows 3 times, then 2nd row once.
11th row Knit to last 3 sts, y fwd, K2 tog (buttonhole), K1.
Rep rows 2 to 11 incl once, then 2nd row once.

SHAPE SHOULDER

Cast off 6 (*6, 7*) sts at beg of next row and foll alt row, then 5 (*7, 7*) sts at beg of foll alt row. Work 1 row.
Leave rem 13 (*14, 14*) sts on a stitch holder.
Join yarn to rem sts, cast on 5 sts for underlap and work to correspond with other side, omitting buttonholes.

Front

Work as for Back to ★★.
Work a further 18 (*20, 20*) rows stocking st.

SHAPE NECK

Next row K22 (*25, 27*), *turn* and cont on these sts.
Dec at neck edge in alt rows until 19 (*20, 23*) sts rem, then in foll 4th row/s until 17 (*19, 21*) sts rem.
Work 1 row.

SHAPE SHOULDER

Cast off 6 (*6, 7*) sts at beg of next row and foll alt row. Work 1 row. Cast off.
Slip next 11 sts onto stitch holder and leave. Join yarn to rem sts and work other side to correspond.

Sleeves

Using 3.00 mm needles, C and knitting-in elastic tog, cast on 41 (*45, 49*) sts.
Work 10 rows rib in stripes as for Back, inc 6 sts evenly across last row... 47 (*51, 55*) sts.
Change to 4.00 mm needles and M only.

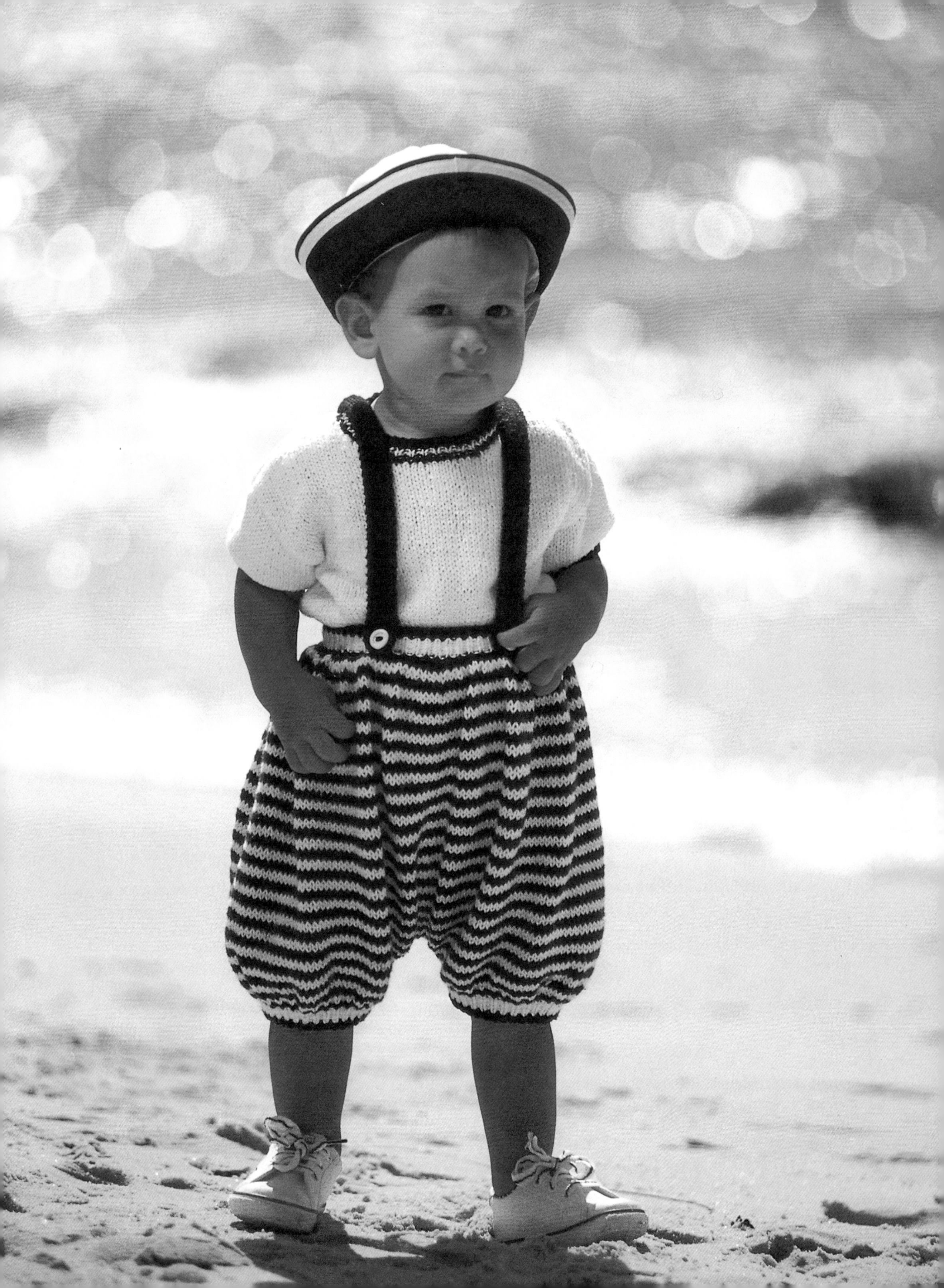

Shorts

Legs

Both alike.

Using 3.00 mm needles, C and knitting-in elastic tog, cast on 61 (67, 69) sts.

Work 9 rows rib as for Back of Jumper, working in stripes of 2 rows C, 6 rows M, then 1 row C.

10th row Using C, rib 9 (2, 0), ★ inc in next st, rib 1, rep from ★ to last st, rib 1 ... 91 (99, 103) sts.

Change to 4.00 mm needles and Stonewash only.

Working in stocking st stripes of 2 rows each M and C throughout, work 4 rows.

SHAPE CROTCH

Cast on 5 (6, 7) sts at beg of next 2 rows ... 101 (111, 117) sts.

Keeping stripes correct, cont until work measures 22 (24, 26) cm from last cast-on sts, ending with a purl row.

Next row K1 (2, 0), ★ (K2 tog) 4 times, K1, rep from ★ to last 1 (1, 0) st/s, K1 (1, 0) ... 57 (63, 65) sts.

Next row Purl.

Change to 3.00 mm needles for **Waistband**.

Work 10 rows rib in stripes as before.

Cast off *loosely* in rib.

Shoulder Straps

Make 2.

Using 3.00 mm needles and C only, cast on 9 sts.

Work 4 rows rib as before.

5th row Rib 4, y fwd, K2 tog, rib 3 ... buttonhole.

Cont in rib until work measures 34 (38, 40) cm from beg.

Cast off *loosely* in rib.

Make up

With a slightly damp cloth and warm iron, press lightly. Using backstitch, join front, back and crotch seams. Sew shoulder straps in position at back, then sew buttons on front waistband. Thread length of round elastic through 2nd, 5th and 8th rows of waistband and draw up to desired measurement. Press seams.

Work in stocking st until work measures 8 (8, 9) cm from beg, ending with a purl row.

Cast off 4 sts at beg of next 10 rows. Cast off rem sts.

Neckband

Using backstitch, join shoulder seams. With right side facing, using 3.00 mm needles and C, knit up 77 (83, 83) sts evenly around neck, incl sts from stitch holders.

1st row (wrong side) K5, ★ P1, K1, rep from ★ to last 4 sts, K4.

2nd row Using M, K6, ★ P1, K1, rep from ★ to last 5 sts, K2, y fwd, K2 tog, K1 ... buttonhole.

Keeping garter edge correct, work 3 rows rib in stripes of 1 more row M, then 2 rows C. Cast off *loosely* in rib.

Make up

With a slightly damp cloth and warm iron, press lightly. Using backstitch, join sleeve and side seams to coloured threads. Sew in sleeves. Sew underlap in position. Sew on buttons. Press seams.

Curly locks, curly locks

Garter stitch on stocking stitch gives the interesting striped pattern on this raglan sleeved jumper

MEASUREMENTS

This garment is designed to be a generous fit.

Size		A	B	C	D
Approx age	months	3	6	12	18
Fits underarm	cm	40	45	50	52.5
	ins	16	18	20	21
Garment measures	cm	*45*	*51*	*56*	*60.5*
Length	cm	24	27	31	33.5
Sleeve fits (approx)	cm	13	16	19	21

MATERIALS

Patons Bluebell 5 Ply *or* Patons 5 Ply Machinewash 50 g balls

Main colour (M)	2	2	3	3
Contrast (C)	1	1	1	1

ACCESSORIES

1 pair each 3.75 mm (no. 9) and 3.00 mm (no. 11) Milward knitting needles or sizes needed to give correct tension, 2 stitch holders, 8 buttons.

TENSION

26.5 sts to 10 cm in width over stocking st, using 3.75 mm needles.

Please check your tension carefully. If less sts use smaller needles, if more sts use bigger needles.

Back

Using 3.00 mm needles and C, cast on 61 (69, 75, 81) sts.

1st row K2, ★ P1, K1, rep from ★ to last st, K1.

2nd row K1, ★ P1, K1, rep from ★ to end.

Rep 1st and 2nd rows 5 times... 12 rows rib in all.

Change to 3.75 mm needles.

Using M, work 10 rows stocking st.

Using C, knit 2 rows garter st.

Last 12 rows form patt.

Cont in patt until work measures 13 (15, *18*, 20) cm from beg, working last row on wrong side.

SHAPE RAGLAN ARMHOLES

Keeping patt correct, cast off 3 sts at beg of next 2 rows. ★★

Dec at each end of next and foll 4th (4th, *alt*, every) row/s until 49 (59, 25, 65) sts rem. **Sizes A, B and D only**, then in alt rows until 23 (*25*, 25) sts rem. **All sizes**, work 1 row.

Leave rem sts on a stitch holder.

Front

Work as for Back to ★★.

Keeping patt correct, dec at each end of next and foll 4th (4th, *alt*, every) row/s until 49 (59, 41, 65) sts rem. **Sizes A, B and D only**, then in alt rows until 37 (41, 41) sts rem. **All sizes**, work 1 row.

SHAPE NECK

Next row K2 tog, patt 11 (13, *13*, 13), turn and cont on these 12 (14, *14*, 14) sts.

Dec at each end of alt rows until 4 sts rem, then at armhole edge only in alt rows until 2 sts rem.

Next row P2, *turn*, K2 tog. Fasten off.

Slip next 11 sts onto stitch holder and leave. Join yarn to rem sts and work other side to correspond.

Sleeves

Using 3.00 mm needles and C, cast on 33 (35, 37, 39) sts.

Work 12 rows rib as for Back, inc 4 (4, 6, 6) sts evenly across last row... 37 (39, *43*, 45) sts.

Change to 3.75 mm needles.

Work 4 rows patt as for Back.

5th row K2, "M1", knit to last 2 sts, "M1", K2.

Cont in patt as for Back, inc (as before) at each end of foll 6th (8th, *10th*, 10th) rows until there are 47 (49, *53*, 57) sts.

Cont without shaping until work measures approx 13 (16, *19*, 21) cm from beg, ending with same patt row as Back and Front at armholes.

SHAPE RAGLAN

Keeping patt correct, cast off 3 sts at beg of next 2 rows.

Dec at each end of next and foll 4th

rows until 37 (37, 41, 47) sts rem, then in alt rows until 7 sts rem.
Work 1 row. Cast off.

Back Neckband

Using backstitch, join back raglan seams, noting that tops of Sleeves form part of neckline. With right side facing, using 3.00 mm needles and C, knit up 37 (39, 39, 39) sts evenly around neck, incl sts from stitch holder. Work 7 rows rib as for Back, beg with a 2nd row. Cast off *loosely* in rib.

Front Neckband

With right side facing, using 3.00 mm needles and C, knit up 37 (43, 43, 43) sts evenly around neck, incl sts from stitch holder.
Work 7 rows rib as for Back, beg with a 2nd row. Cast off *loosely* in rib.

Right Front Opening Band

Using backstitch, join front raglan seam for 2 cm. With right side facing, using 3.00 mm needles and C, knit up 41 (45, 49, 51) sts evenly along front raglan edge (incl end of Neckband).
Work 1 row rib as for Back, as 2nd row. ★★★
2nd row Rib 3, [cast off 2 sts, rib 8 (9, 10, 11)] 3 times, cast off 2 sts, rib 6 (7, 8, 7).
3rd row Rib 6 (7, 8, 7), [*turn*, cast on 2 sts, *turn*, rib 8 (9, 10, 11)] 3 times, *turn*, cast on 2 sts, *turn*, rib 3… 4 buttonholes.
Work 2 rows rib. Cast off *loosely* in rib.

Left Front Opening Band

Work as for Right Front Opening Band to ★★★.
2nd row Rib 6 (7, 8, 7), [cast off 2 sts, rib 8 (9, 10, 11)] 3 times, cast off 2 sts, rib 3.
3rd row Rib 3, [*turn*, cast on 2 sts, *turn*, rib 8 (9, 10, 11)] 3 times, *turn*, cast on 2 sts, *turn*, rib 6 (7, 8, 7)… 4 buttonholes.
Work 2 rows rib. Cast off *loosely* in rib.

Continued on page 109

Sugar and spice

Create a delightful picture with a butterfly eyelet pattern and soft pastel embroidered flowers on white cotton

MEASUREMENTS — SINGLET AND BLOOMERS

The singlet is designed to be a neat fit.

Size		A	B	C	D
Approx age	months	12	18	24	36
SINGLET					
Fits underarm	cm	50	52.5	55	57.5
	ins	20	21	22	23
Garment measures	cm	52	54.5	57	59.5
Length	cm	21	23	25	27
BLOOMERS					
Outside leg length	cm	30	32	34	36

MATERIALS

Patons Stonewash Cotton 8 Ply 50 g balls

Singlet	2	3	3	4
Bloomers	4	4	4	5

ACCESSORIES

1 pair each 4.00 mm (no. 8) and 3.00 mm (no. 11) Milward knitting needles or sizes needed to give correct tension, 2 stitch holders and 4 contrasting colours in Stonewash Cotton for embroidery for Singlet, length of round elastic for Bloomers.

TENSION

22 sts to 10 cm in width over stocking st, using 4.00 mm needles.
Please check your tension carefully. If less sts use smaller needles, if more sts use bigger needles.

Singlet

Back

Using 4.00 mm needles, cast on 89 (93, 99, 103) sts.
Knit 5 rows garter st (1st row is wrong side).
Work 6 rows stocking st.
Next row K5 (3, 3, 1), ★ K2 tog, K1, rep from ★ to end... 61 (63, 67, 69) sts.
Purl 1 row.

BEG PATT

1st row K10 (11, 13, 14), ★ K2 tog, y fwd, K1, y fwd, sl 1, K1, psso, K13, rep from ★ ending last rep with K10 (11, 13, 14) instead of K13.
2nd row P12 (13, 15, 16), ★ sl 1 purlways, P17, rep from ★ ending last rep with P12 (13, 15, 16) instead of P17.
Rep 1st and 2nd rows once.
Work 8 rows stocking st.
13th row K1 (2, 4, 5), ★ K2 tog, y fwd, K1, y fwd, sl 1, k1, psso, K13, rep from ★ ending last rep with K1 (2, 4, 5) instead of K13.
14th row P3 (4, 6, 7), ★ sl 1 purlways, P17, rep from ★ ending last rep with P3 (4, 6, 7) instead of P17.
Rep 13th and 14th rows once.
Work 8 rows stocking st.
Last 24 rows form patt.
Cont in patt until work measures 10 (11.5, 13, 14.5) cm from dec row, working last row on wrong side.

SHAPE ARMHOLES

Keeping patt correct, cast off 4 sts at beg of next 2 rows.
Dec at each end of next and alt rows until 43 (45, 49, 51) sts rem. ★★
Work a further 11 (13, 15, 15) rows patt.

SHAPE NECK

Next row Patt 13 (14, 15, 16), *turn* and cont on these sts.
Dec at neck edge in alt rows until 10 (11, 12, 13) sts rem.
Work 3 rows patt. Cast off.
Slip next 17 (17, 19, 19) sts onto a stitch holder and leave. Join yarn to rem sts and work other side to correspond.

Front

Work as for Back to ★★.
Work a further 3 (5, 5, 5) rows patt.

SHAPE NECK

Patt 17 (18, 20, 21), *turn* and cont on these sts.
Keeping patt correct, dec at neck edge only in alt rows until 10 (11, 12, 13) sts rem.
Work 3 rows patt. Cast off rem sts.
Slip next 9 sts onto stitch holder and leave. Join yarn to rem sts and work other side to correspond.

Neckband

Using backstitch, join right shoulder seam. With right side facing and using 3.00 mm needles, knit up 74 (74, 80, 80) sts evenly around neck, incl sts from stitch holders.
Knit 6 rows garter st. Cast off.

Armhole Bands

Using backstitch, join left shoulder seam. With right side facing and using

3.00 mm needles, knit up 56 (58, 60, 64) sts evenly along armhole edge. Knit 6 rows garter st. Cast off.

Make up

Using Knitting Stitch (see page 40) and contrasting colours as illustrated, embroider flowers from graphs (see below left). With a slightly damp cloth and warm iron, press lightly, taking care not to flatten patt. Using backstitch, join side seams. Press seams.

Bloomers

Legs

Both alike.

Using 4.00 mm needles, cast on 99 (103, 105, 109) sts.

Knit 5 rows garter st (1st row is wrong side).

Work 6 rows stocking st.

12th row K3 (1, 3, 1), ★ K2 tog, K1, rep from ★ to end... 67 (69, 71, 73) sts.

13th row Purl.

14th row K3 (1, 3, 1), ★ inc in next st, K1, rep from ★ to end... 99 (103, 105, 109) sts.

Work 3 rows stocking st (beg with a purl row).

SHAPE CROTCH

Cast on 6 (7, 8, 9) sts at beg of next 2 rows... 111 (117, 123, 129) sts.

Cont in stocking st until work measures 24 (26, 28, 30) cm from last cast-on sts, ending with a purl row.

Next row K8 (6, 6, 4), ★ K2 tog, rep from ★ to last 7 (7, 5, 5) sts, K7 (7, 5, 5)... 63 (65, 67, 69) sts.

Next row Purl.

Change to 3.00 mm needles for **Waistband**.

Knit 11 rows garter st. Cast off *loosely*.

Make up

With a slightly damp cloth and warm iron, press lightly. Using backstitch, join front, back and crotch seams. Thread length of round elastic through legs at dec row and through 2nd, 6th and 10th rows of waistband and draw up to desired measurement. Press seams.

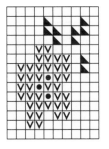 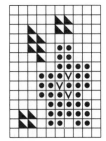

Key for Knitting Stitch embroidery
☑ Blue   ⊡ Pink   ◩ Yellow   ◨ Mint

MEASUREMENTS — EMBROIDERED CARDIGAN OR JUMPER

This garment is designed to be a generous fit.

Size		A	B	C	D
Approx age	months	12	18	24	36
Fits underarm	cm	50	52.5	55	57.5
	ins	20	21	22	23
Garment measures	*cm*	*54*	*57*	*60*	*63*
Length	cm	25	27	29	31
Sleeve fits	cm	19	21	23	25
(or length desired)					

MATERIALS

Patons Stonewash Cotton 8 Ply 50 g balls

Cardigan or Jumper	3	3	4	4

ACCESSORIES

1 pair each 4.00 mm (no. 8) and 3.00 mm (no. 11) Milward knitting needles or sizes needed to give correct tension, 1 stitch holder, 4 contrasting colours in Stonewash Cotton for embroidery, 4 buttons.

TENSION

22 sts to 10 cm in width over stocking st, using 4.00 mm needles.
Please check your tension carefully. If less sts use smaller needles, if more sts use bigger needles.

Cardigan

Back

Using 4.00 mm needles, cast on 91 (97, *103*, 105) sts.
Knit 5 rows garter st (1st row is wrong side).
Work 7 rows stocking st.
Next row P1, ★ P2 tog, P1, rep from ★ to last 0 (0, *0*, 2) sts, P0 (0, *0*, 2)... 61 (65, *69*, 71) sts.

BEG PATT

1st row K10 (12, *14*, 15), ★ K2 tog, y fwd, K1, y fwd, sl 1, K1, psso, K13, rep from ★ ending last rep with K10 (12, *14*, 15) instead of K13.
2nd row P12 (14, *16*, 17), ★ sl 1 purlways, P17, rep from ★ ending last rep with P12 (14, *16*, 17) instead of P17.
Rep 1st and 2nd rows once.
Work 8 rows stocking st.
13th row K1 (3, *5*, 6), ★ K2 tog, y fwd, K1, y fwd, sl 1, K1, psso, K13, rep from ★ ending last rep with K1 (3, *5*, 6) instead of K13.
14th row P3 (5, *7*, 8), ★ sl 1 purlways, P17, rep from ★ ending last rep with P3 (5, *7*, 8) instead of P17.
Rep 13th and 14th rows once.

Work 8 rows stocking st.
Last 24 rows form patt.
Cont in patt until work measures 23.5 (25.5, *27.5*, 29.5) cm from beg, working last row on wrong side.

SHAPE SHOULDERS

Keeping patt correct, cast off 5 (5, *6*, 6) sts at beg of next 6 rows, then 4 (6, *4*, 5) sts at beg of foll 2 rows.
Leave rem 23 (23, *25*, 25) sts on a stitch holder.

Left Front

Using 4.00 mm needles, cast on 47 (49, *51*, 53) sts.
Knit 5 rows garter st (1st row is wrong side).
Work 7 rows stocking st.
Next row P2 (3, *8*, 4), ★ (P2 tog) 2 (2, *1*, 2) time/s, P1 (1, *0*, 1), rep from ★ to last 5 (6, *9*, 4) sts, P2 (2, *0*, 0) tog, P3 (4, *3*, 4)... 30 (32, *34*, 35) sts.

BEG PATT

1st row K10 (12, *14*, 15), K2 tog, y fwd, K1, y fwd, sl 1, K1, psso, knit to end.

2nd row P17, sl 1 purlways, purl to end.

Rep 1st and 2nd rows once.

Cont in patt as for Back, *as placed* in last 4 rows, until there are 9 (9, *11*, 11) rows less than Back to shoulder shaping, working last row on right side.

SHAPE NECK

Keeping patt correct, cast off 5 (5, *5*, 6) sts at beg of next row.

Dec at neck edge in every row until 20 (22, *24*, 26) sts rem, then in alt row/s until 19 (21, *22*, 23) sts rem. Work 1 row patt.

SHAPE SHOULDER

Cast off 5 (5, *6*, 6) sts at beg of next and alt rows 3 times in all. Work 1 row, Cast off.

Right Front

Work to correspond with Left Front.

Sleeves

Using 3.00 mm needles, cast on 39 (41, *41*, 43) sts.

Knit 5 rows garter st (1st row is wrong side).

Change to 4.00 mm needles.

BEG PATT

1st row K8 (9, *9*, 10), ★ K2 tog, y fwd, K1, y fwd, sl 1, K1, psso, K13, rep from ★ ending last rep with K8 (9, *9*, 10) instead of K13.

2nd row P10 (11, *11*, 12), ★ sl 1 purlways, P17, rep from ★ ending last rep with P10 (11, *11*, 12) instead of P17.

Rep 1st and 2nd rows once.

Keeping patt correct as for Back, *as placed* in last 4 rows, and working extra sts into patt as they become available, inc at each end of next and foll 4th (4th, *4th*, 6th) rows until there are 49 (45, *45*, 57) sts, then in foll 6th (6th, *6th*, 8th) row/s until there are 53 (55, *57*, 59) sts.

Cont without shaping until work measures 17 (19, *21*, 23) cm (or 2 cm less than desired length to allow for loose fit) from beg, working last row on wrong side.

Cast off 6 sts at beg of next 6 rows. Cast off rem sts.

Neckband

Using backstitch, join shoulder seams. With right side facing and using 3.00 mm needles, knit up 69 (69, *77*, 77) sts evenly around neck, incl sts from stitch holder. Knit 6 rows garter st. Cast off.

Left Front Band

Using 3.00 mm needles, cast on 46 (52, *58*, 61) sts.

Knit 2 rows garter st.

3rd row K4, ★ cast off 2 sts, K10 (12, *14*, 15), rep from ★ to last 6 sts, cast off 2 sts, K4.

4th row K4, ★ *turn*, cast on 2 sts, *turn*, K10 (12, *14*, 15), rep from ★ to last 4 sts, *turn*, cast on 2 sts, *turn*, K4… 4 buttonholes.

Knit 2 rows garter st. Cast off.

Right Front Band

Work as for Left Front Band, omitting buttonholes.

Make up

Using Knitting Stitch (see page 40) and contrasting colours as illustrated, embroider flowers from graphs (see page 60). With a slightly damp cloth and warm iron, press lightly, taking care not to flatten patt. Tie a coloured thread at side edges of back and fronts 12 (13.5, *15*, 16.5) cm up from lower edge to mark position of armholes. Using backstitch, join sleeve and side seams to coloured threads. Sew in sleeves. Sew front bands in position. Sew on buttons. Press seams.

Jumper

Back and Sleeves

Work as for Cardigan, casting off back neck sts instead of leaving on stitch holder.

Front

Work as for Back until there are 10

(10, *12*, 12) rows less than Back to shoulder shaping, working last row on wrong side.

SHAPE NECK

Next row Patt 23 (25, *26*, 27), *turn* and cont on these sts. Keeping patt correct, dec at neck edge in alt rows until 19 (21, *22*, 23) sts rem. Work 1 (1, *3*, 3) row/s patt.

SHAPE SHOULDER

Keeping patt correct, cast off 5 (5, *6*,

6) sts at beg of next and alt rows 3 times in all. Work 1 row. Cast off. Slip next 15 (15, 17, 17) sts onto stitch holder and leave. Join yarn to rem sts and work other side to correspond.

Front Neckband

With right side facing and using 3.00 mm needles, knit up 79 (83, 91, 97) sts evenly along shoulders and neckline, incl sts from stitch holder. Knit 6 rows garter st. Cast off.

Make up

Using Knitting Stitch (see page 40) and contrasting colours as illustrated, embroider flowers from graphs (see page 60). With a slightly damp cloth and warm iron, press lightly, taking care not to flatten patt. Tie a coloured thread at side edges of back and front 12 (13.5, 15, 16.5) cm up from lower edge to mark position of armholes. Using backstitch, join shoulder seams for 4.5 (5, 5.5, 6) cm. Join sleeve and side seams to coloured threads. Sew in sleeves. Make 2 buttonloops on each front shoulder and sew on buttons to correspond. Press seams.

Little Tommy Tittlemouse

Zipper up your little one in this warm Feathersoft Fair Isle jacket with its cosy hood and matching socks

MEASUREMENTS
The jacket is designed to be a generous fit.

Size		A	B	C	D	E
Approx age	months	3	6	12	18	24
JACKET						
Fits underarm	cm	40	45	50	52.5	55
	ins	16	18	20	21	22
Garment measures	cm	44	48.5	55	58	61
Length	cm	29	29	34.5	34.5	35
Sleeve fits	cm	13	16	19	21	23
(or length desired)						
SOCKS						
Fit foot (approx)	cm	8	9.5	11	12.5	14

MATERIALS
Patons Feathersoft 4 Ply 25 g balls

		A	B	C	D	E
JACKET						
Main colour (M)		5	5	6	6	7
Contrast (C)		1	1	1	2	2
SOCKS						
Main colour (M)		1	1	1	1	1
Contrast (C)		small quantity for each size				

ACCESSORIES
1 pair each 3.25 mm (no. 10), 3.75 mm (no. 9) and 2.75 mm (no. 12) Milward knitting needles or sizes needed to give correct tension, 25 (25,30,30,30) cm Opti-lon Jacket zipper, 2 stitch holders for Socks.

TENSION
29 sts to 10 cm in width over stocking st, using 3.25 mm needles.
Please check your tension carefully. If less sts use smaller needles, if more sts use bigger needles.

Jacket

Back
Using 2.75 mm needles and C, cast on 65 (73,81,85,89) sts.
1st row K2, ★ P1, K1, rep from ★ to last st, K1.
2nd row K1, ★ P1, K1, rep from ★ to end.

Rep 1st and 2nd rows 5 times, working 8 rows M, then 2 rows C... 12 rows rib in all.
Change to 3.25 mm needles and M.
Work 2 rows in stocking st.
Change to 3.75 mm needles.
Note In Fair Isle patt, **do not weave** colours but carry colour not in use *loosely* across on wrong side. It is important, however, that no colour should be carried across more than 7 sts, and where this is necessary it should be woven under and over colour in use at centre st. Always carry colours to ends of rows and always carry M above C.
Work rows 1 to 9 incl from graph (see page 66).
Change to 3.25 mm needles.
Work 4 rows stocking st (beg with a purl row), working 2 rows each M and C.
Using M for rem, cont in stocking st until work measures 17.5 (17.5,21, 21, 21) cm from beg, ending with a purl row.

SHAPE RAGLAN ARMHOLES
Cast off 2 (3,3,3,3) sts at beg of next 2 rows.
Dec at each end of next and alt rows until 21 (23,29,33,35) sts rem. **Sizes C, D and E only**, then in every row until (23,23,25) sts rem. **All sizes**, work 1 (1,0,0,0) row/s stocking st.
Cast off rem sts.

Left Front
Using 2.75 mm needles and C, cast on 33 (37,41,43,45) sts.
Work 12 rows rib in stripes as for Back.

Change to 3.25 mm needles.
Using M, work 2 rows stocking st.
Change to 3.75 mm needles.
Work rows 1 to 9 incl from graph.
Change to 3.25 mm needles.

Work 4 rows stocking st (beg with a purl row), working 2 rows each M and C.

Using M for rem, cont in stocking st until work measures same as Back to armholes, ending with a purl row.

SHAPE RAGLAN ARMHOLE

Cast off 2 (3,3,3,3) sts at beg of next row.

Work 1 row.

Dec at beg of next and alt rows until 18 (19,22,23,25) sts rem.

SHAPE NECK

Cast off 4 (5,5,5,5) sts at beg of next row.

Dec at each end of next and alt rows until 4 (4,7,8,8) sts rem.

Dec at armhole edge only in alt row/s until 2 (2,5,7,7) sts rem. **Sizes C, D and E only**, then in every row until 2 sts rem. **All sizes**, work 1 (1,0,0,0) row/s stocking st.

Next row K2 tog. Fasten off.

Right Front

Work to correspond with Left Front.

Sleeves

Using 2.75 mm needles and C, cast on 37 (39,39,43,43) sts.

Work 12 rows rib as for Back, inc 8 (6,10,10,10) sts evenly across last row... 45 (45,49,53,53) sts.

Change to 3.25 mm needles.

Using M, work 2 rows stocking st.

Change to 3.75 mm needles.

Work rows 1 to 9 incl from graph as for Size D (D,A,D,D) of Back.

Change to 3.25 mm needles.

Using M, work 2 rows stocking st (beg with a purl row), inc at each end of 2nd row.

Using C, work 2 rows stocking st.

Using M for rem, inc at each end of foll 6th (8th,12th,8th,8th) row/s from previous inc until there are 49 (51,55,59,61) sts, then in foll 8th (10th,14th,10th,10th) row/s until there are 51 (53,57,65,67) sts.

Cont without shaping until work measures 13 (16,19,21,23) cm (or length desired) from beg, ending with a purl row.

SHAPE RAGLAN ARMHOLES

Cast off 2 (3,3,3,3) sts at beg of next 2 rows.

Dec at each end of next and foll 4th rows until 41 (37,41,55,57) sts rem, then in alt rows until 11 sts rem.

Work 1 row. Cast off.

Hood

Using 2.75 mm needles and C, cast on 107 (123,137,145,153) sts.

Work 18 rows rib as for Back, working 2 rows C, 14 rows M, then 2 rows C.

Change to 3.25 mm needles and M for rem.

Work in stocking st until work measures 13.5 (14,14.5,14.5,15) cm from centre row of rib band, ending with a purl row.

SHAPE BACK

Cast off 6 sts at beg of next 10 (12,14,16,16) rows.

Cast off rem sts.

Front Bands

Make 2.

Using 2.75 mm needles and C, cast on 67 (69,81,85,87) sts.

Work 12 rows rib in stripes as for Back.

Cast off *loosely* in rib.

Make up

Do not press. Using backstitch, join raglan, side and sleeve seams. Fold hood band in half onto wrong side and slipstitch in position. Sew cast-off edge of front bands in position. Join centre back seam of hood, then sew hood in position, leaving outside of hem edge free to thread cord through. Sew in zipper. Using 3 strands of C, 3 metres long, make a twisted cord (see below) and thread through casing of hood. Tie a knot 2.5 cm from each end of cord and cut ends to form tassels.

TO MAKE A TWISTED CORD

Method requires two people. Take as many strands of yarn as required, approximately three times the length required for the finished cord. Knot each end and slip a pencil between strands. Each person holds yarn just below pencil with one hand and twists pencil clockwise with other hand, keeping yarn taut (A). When yarn begins to kink, catch centre over door-knob or back of chair (B). Bring pencils together for one person to hold, while other grasps centre of yarn, sliding hand down and releasing at short intervals, letting yarn twist (C). Knot ends to prevent unravelling.

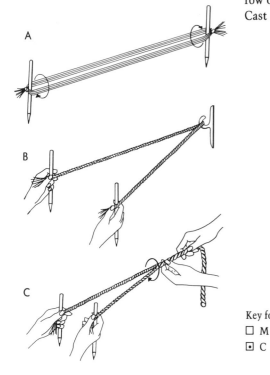

Socks

Using 2.75 mm needles and M, cast on 41 (41,45,45,45) sts.
Work 4 rows rib as for Back of Jacket.
Change to 3.25 mm needles.
Using C, work 2 rows stocking st.
Using M, work 2 rows stocking st.
Change to 3.75 mm needles.
Work rows 1 to 9 incl from graph as for Size A (A,D,D,D) of Back.
Change to 3.25 mm needles.
Using M for rem, work 2 rows stocking st (beg with a purl row), dec 0 (0,2,2,2) sts evenly (purlways) across 1st row ... 41 (41,43,43,43) sts.
Work in stocking st until work measures 8 (9,10,11,12) cm from beg, ending with a purl row. Break off yarn.
Slip first 11 (11,12,12,12) sts onto a stitch holder. Join yarn to rem sts.
Next row K3, K2 tog, K9, K2 tog, K3, *turn*.
Leave rem 11 (11,12,12,12) sts on second stitch holder.
Work 19 (23,25,27,29) rows stocking st on these 17 sts (beg with a purl row).

SHAPE TOE

1st row K2, sl 1, K1, psso, knit to last 4 sts, K2 tog, K2.
2nd row Purl.
Rep 1st and 2nd rows once, then 1st row once ... 11 sts.
Cast off.

SHAPE HEEL

With wrong side facing, slip 11 (11,12,12,12) sts from first stitch holder onto a 3.25 mm needle, then slip 11 (11,12,12,12) sts from second stitch holder onto same needle (ending at inside edge) ... 22 (22,24,24,24) sts.
With right side facing, rejoin yarn.
Next row K1, (K2 tog) twice, K5 (5,6,6,6), K2 tog, K5 (5,6,6,6), (K2 tog) twice, K1 ... 17 (17,19,19,19) sts.
Work 5 rows stocking st (beg with a purl row).

TURN HEEL

Note When turning, bring yarn to front of work, slip next st onto right-hand needle, y bk, slip st back onto left-hand needle, then *turn* and proceed as instructed — this avoids holes in work.

1st row K12 (12,14,14,14), *turn*.
2nd row P7 (7,9,9,9), *turn*.
3rd row K8 (8,10,10,10), *turn*.
4th row P9 (9,11,11,11), *turn*.
5th row K10 (10,12,12,12), *turn*.
6th row P11 (11,13,13,13), *turn*.
7th row K12 (12,14,14,14), *turn*.
8th row P13 (13,15,15,15), *turn*.
9th row K14 (14,16,16,16), *turn*.
10th row P15 (15,17,17,17), *turn*.
11th row Knit to end.
12th row Purl to end.
Break off yarn.

Continued on page 109

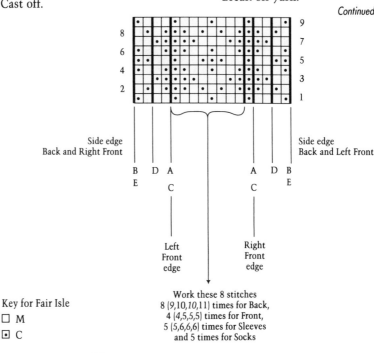

Key for Fair Isle
☐ M
⊡ C

Side edge
Back and Right Front

Side edge
Back and Left Front

B D A   A D B
E   C   C   E

Left Front edge

Right Front edge

Work these 8 stitches
8 (9,10,10,11) times for Back,
4 (4,5,5,5) times for Front,
5 (5,6,6,6) times for Sleeves
and 5 times for Socks

Oranges and lemons

MEASUREMENTS

This garment is designed to be a generous fit.

Size		A	B	C	D
Approx age	months	12	18	24	36
Fits underarm	cm	50	52.5	55	57.5
	ins	20	21	22	23
Garment measures	cm	56	59.5	63	66.5
Length	cm	33	36	38	40
Sleeve fits	cm	19	21	23	25
(or length desired)					

MATERIALS

Patons Stonewash Cotton 8 Ply 50 g balls

Main colour (M)	3	3	4	4
Contrast (C)	1	1	1	1

ACCESSORIES

1 pair each 4.00 mm (no. 8), 4.50 mm (no. 7) and 3.00 mm (no. 11) Milward knitting needles or sizes needed to give correct tension, knitting-in elastic, 1 stitch holder, 3 buttons.

TENSION

22 sts to 10 cm in width over stocking st, using 4.00 mm needles.
Please check your tension carefully. If less sts use smaller needles, if more sts use bigger needles.

Stripes and checks combine on this Stonewash Cotton jumper to achieve a striking effect

Back

Using 3.00 mm needles, M and knitting-in elastic tog, cast on 63 (67,71,75) sts.

1st row K2, ★ P1, K1, rep from ★ to last st, K1.

2nd row K1, ★ P1, K1, rep from ★ to end.

Rep 1st and 2nd rows until work measures 3 (3,4,4) cm from beg, ending with a 2nd row and inc once in centre of last row... 64 (68,72,76) sts.

Change to 4.00 mm needles and Stonewash only.

Work in stocking st in stripes of 2 rows C, 10 rows M throughout, until work measures 20 (22.5,24,25.5) cm from beg, ending with a purl row.

Tie a coloured thread at each end of last row to mark beg of armholes as there is no armhole shaping. ★★

BEG CHECK PATT

Using M, work 2 rows stocking st.

Change to 4.50 mm needles.

Note In Fair Isle patt, **do not weave** colours but carry colour not in use *loosely* across on wrong side. Always carry colours to ends of rows and always carry M above C.

3rd row K4 (0,2,4)M, ★ K2C, K4M, rep from ★ to last 0 (2,4,0) sts, K0 (2,2,0)C, K0 (0,2,0)M.

4th row Purl in same colours as previous row.

Change to 4.00 mm needles.

Using M, work 4 rows stocking st.

Change to 4.50 mm needles.

9th row K1 (3,0,1)M, K2 (2,1,2)C, ★ K4M, K2C, rep from ★ to last 1 (3,5,1) st/s, K1 (3,4,1)M, K0 (0,1,0)C.

10th row Purl in same colours as previous row.

Change to 4.00 mm needles.

Using M, work 2 rows stocking st.

Last 12 rows form check patt.

Work a further 22(24,26,26) rows patt.

SHAPE SHOULDERS

Keeping patt correct, cast off 6 (6,7,7) sts at beg of next 6 rows, then 5 (7,5,7) sts at beg of foll 2 rows.

Leave rem 18 (18,20,20) sts on stitch holder.

Front

Work as for Back to ★★.

DIVIDE FOR FRONT OPENING AND BEG CHECK PATT

1st row Using M, K30 (32,34,36), cast off 4 sts, knit to end.

Cont on last 30 (32,34,36) sts.

2nd row Using M, purl.

Change to 4.50 mm needles.

3rd row ★ K2C, K4M, rep from ★ to last 0 (2,4,0) sts, K0 (2,2,0)C, K0 (0,2,0)M.

4th row Purl in same colours as previous row.

Change to 4.00 mm needles.

Using M, work 4 rows stocking st.

Change to 4.50 mm needles.

9th row K3M, ★ K2C, K4M, rep from ★ to last 3 (5,1,3) st/s, K2 (2,1,2)C, K1 (3,0,1)M.

10th row Purl in same colours as previous row.

Change to 4.00 mm needles.

Using M, work 3 rows stocking st.

Last 12 rows form check patt.

Work a further 11 (13,13,13) rows patt.

SHAPE NECK

Keeping patt correct, cast off 4 sts at beg of next row.

Dec at neck edge in alt rows until 23 (25,26,28) sts rem.

Work 4 rows patt.

SHAPE SHOULDER

Cast off 6 (6,7,7) sts at beg of next and alt rows 3 times in all.

Work 1 row. Cast off.

Join yarn to rem 30 (32,34,36) sts and work other side to correspond.

Sleeves

Using 3.00 mm needles, M and knitting-in elastic tog, cast on 31 (33,33,35) sts.

Work 3 (3,4,4) cm in rib as for Back, inc 8 sts evenly across last row... 39 (41,41,43) sts.

Change to 4.00 mm needles and Stonewash only.

Working in striped patt as for Back throughout, work 4 rows.

5th row K2, "M1", knit to last 2 sts, "M1", K2.

Keeping striped patt correct, inc (as before) at each end of foll 6th rows until there are 53 (55,57,59) sts.

Cont without shaping until work measures 19 (21,23,25) cm (or length desired) from beg, ending with a purl row.

Using M for rem, cast off 4 (4,5,5) sts at beg of next 8 rows.

Cast off rem sts.

Left Front Band

Using 3.00 mm needles and M only, cast on 7 sts.

Work 24 (26,26,26) rows rib as for Back. Leave sts on a safety pin, break off yarn.

Right Front Band

Using 3.00 mm needles and M only, cast on 7 sts.

Work 8 (10,10,10) rows rib as for Back.

Next row Rib 3, yrn, P2 tog (buttonhole), rib 2.

Work 16 rows rib, working a buttonhole (as before) in foll 10th row from previous buttonhole... 2 buttonholes.

Leave sts on needle, do not break off yarn.

Neckband

Using backstitch, join shoulder seams. Sew Front Bands in position, lapping right over left at centre front. With right side facing, using 3.00 mm needle holding Right Front Band sts and M only, knit up 57 (57,63,63) sts evenly around neck, incl sts from stitch holder, then rib across Left Front Band sts... 71 (71,77,77) sts.

Continued on page 110

Jack and Jill

Buttons, stripes and a delicate Fair Isle pattern feature on both the dress and rompers, cool and comfortable outfits for the busy toddler

MEASUREMENTS
These garments are designed to be a generous fit.

Size		A	B	C	D	E
Approx age	months	6	12	18	24	36
Fits underarm	cm	45	50	52.5	55	57.5
	ins	18	20	21	22	23
Garments measure (at armhole)	cm	*50*	*55*	*58*	*60.5*	*63.5*
DRESS						
Length	cm	32.5	36.5	40.5	44	48
ROMPERS						
Length	cm	38	41	44	43	47

MATERIALS
Patons Stonewash Cotton 8 Ply 50 g balls

DRESS					
Main colour (M)	1	1	1	1	2
Contrast (C)	3	3	4	4	4
ROMPERS					
Main colour (M)	2	3	3	4	4
Contrast (C)	1	2	2	2	2

ACCESSORIES
1 pair each 4.00 mm (no. 8) and 3.00 mm (no. 11) Milward knitting needles or sizes needed to give correct tension, 1 stitch holder, 4 buttons for Dress, knitting-in elastic and 7 buttons for Rompers.

TENSION
22 sts and 29 rows to 10 cm over stocking st, using 4.00 mm needles.
Please check your tension carefully. If less sts use smaller needles, if more sts use bigger needles.

Dress

Skirt
Make 2.
Using 3.00 mm needles and C, cast on 103 (113,121,125,131) sts.
Work 6 rows stocking st.
7th row (hem edge) K1, ★ y fwd, K2 tog, rep from ★ to end.

Change to 4.00 mm needles.
Work 5 rows stocking st, beg with a purl row.
Note In Fair Isle patt, **do not weave** colours but carry colour not in use *loosely* across on wrong side. Always carry colours to ends of rows and always carry M above C.

★★ BEG PATT
1st row Using M, knit.
2nd row Using M, purl.
3rd row K0 (5,0,5,5)M, ★K1C, K5M, rep from ★ to last 1 (6,1,6,6) st/s, K1C, K0 (5,0,5,5)M.
Work 4 rows stocking st, beg with a purl row.
8th row P3 (2,3,2,2)M, ★ P1C, P5M, rep from ★ to last 4 (3,4,3,3) sts, P1C, P3 (2,3,2,2)M.
9th and 10th rows As 1st and 2nd rows.
Last 10 rows form patt. ★★
Cont in patt until work measures 21 (24,27,30,33) cm from hem edge, ending with a purl row.
Next row K6 (6,4,6,6), ★ K2 tog, rep from ★ to last 5 (7,5,7,5) sts, K5 (7,5,7,5)... 57 (63,65,69,71) sts.
Next row Purl. Cast off *loosely*.

Back Yoke
Using 4.00 mm needles and C, cast on 47 (53,55,59,61) sts.
Work 34 (36,40,42, 44) rows stocking st in stripes of 2 rows each M and C throughout.

SHAPE SHOULDERS
Keeping stripes correct, cast off 8 (9,9,10,10) sts at beg of next 2 rows, then 7 (8,9,9,10) sts at beg of foll 2 rows... 17 (19,19,21,21) sts.
Change to 3.00 mm needles and M only for **Back Neckband**.
Work 8 rows rib as before. Cast off *loosely* in rib.

Front Yoke
Using 4.00 mm needles and C, cast on 47 (53,55,59,61) sts.
Work 22 (22,26,26,28) rows in stripes as for Back Yoke.

SHAPE NECK
Next row K19 (22,23,25,26), *turn* and cont on these sts.
Keeping stripes correct, dec at neck edge in every row until 15 (18,19,21,22) sts rem. **Sizes B, C, D and E only**, then in alt row/s until (17,18,19,20) sts rem. **All sizes**, work 1 row.
Note There are less rows on front shoulder than on back to allow for Shoulder Bands.

SHAPE SHOULDER

Cast off 8 (9,9,10,10) sts at beg of next row.

Work 1 row. Cast off.

Slip next 9 sts onto stitch holder and leave. Join yarn to rem sts and work other side to correspond.

Front Neckband

With right side facing, using 3.00 mm needles and M, knit up 25 (29,29,33,33) sts evenly around front neck, incl sts from stitch holder.

Work 7 rows rib as before, beg with a 2nd row. Cast off *loosely* in rib.

Left Front Shoulder Band

With right side facing, using 3.00 mm needles and M, knit up 21 (23,25,27,29) sts evenly along left front shoulder, incl end of Neckband.

Work 3 rows rib as before, beg with a 2nd row.

4th row ★ Rib 7 (8,9,10,11), cast off 2 sts, rep from ★ once, rib 3.

5th row Rib 3, ★ *turn*, cast on 2 sts, *turn*, rib 7 (8,9,10,11), rep from ★ once… 2 buttonholes.

Work 2 rows rib. Cast off *loosely* in rib.

Right Front Shoulder Band

Work to correspond with Left Front Shoulder Band.

Back Shoulder Bands

Work as for Front Shoulder Bands, omitting buttonholes.

Armhole Bands

Lap Front Shoulder Bands over Back and oversew tog at armhole edge. With right side facing, using 3.00 mm needles and M, knit up 53 (57,63,65,67) sts evenly along armhole edge.

Work 7 rows rib as before, beg with a 2nd row. Cast off *loosely* in rib.

Make up

With a slightly damp cloth and warm iron, press lightly. Using backstitch, join side seams of skirt. Sew yoke to skirt. Sew on buttons. Press seams.

Rompers

Back and Front Yoke and Bands

Work as for Dress, reversing colours.

Legs

Both alike.

Using 3.00 mm needles, C and knitting-in elastic tog, cast on 61 (67,69,69,71) sts.

1st row K2, ★ P1, K1, rep from ★ to last st, K1.

2nd row K1, ★ P1, K1, rep from ★ to end.

Rep 1st and 2nd rows twice, then 1st row once.

8th row Rib 6 (8,8,6,8), ★ inc in each of next 2 sts, rib 1, rep from ★ to last 7 (8,7,6,6) sts, rib to end … 93 (101,105, 107,109) sts.

Change to 4.50 mm needles and Stone-wash only.

Using M, work 3 rows stocking st.

Next row P4 (2,1,5,3)M, ★ P1C, P5M, rep from ★ to last 5 (3,2,6,4) sts, P1C, P4 (2,1,5,3)M.

SHAPE CROTCH

Using M, cast on 5 (6,8,9,11) sts at beg of next 2 rows … 103 (113,121, 125,131) sts.

Work in patt as from ★★ to ★★ for Skirt of Dress until work measures 22 (24,26,24.5,27.5) cm from last cast-on sts, ending with a purl row.

Next row K6 (6,4,6,6), ★ K2 tog, rep from ★ to last 5 (7,5,7,5) sts, knit to end… 57 (63,65,69,71) sts.

Next row Purl. Cast off *loosely*.

Make up

With a slightly damp cloth and warm iron, press lightly. Using backstitch, join front and back seams of leg pieces tog. Sew yoke to legs, placing leg seams to centre back and front of yoke, and catching yoke pieces tog at sides.

Front Leg Opening Band

With right side facing, using 3.00 mm needles and C, knit up 26 (28,30,32,34) sts evenly along front edge of leg opening.

Knit 1 row.

2nd row K3, ★ cast off 2 sts, K7 (8,9,10,11), rep from ★ once, cast off 2 sts, K3.

3rd row K3, ★ *turn*, cast on 2 sts, *turn*, K7 (8,9,10,11), rep from ★ once, *turn*, cast on 2 sts, *turn*, K3… 3 buttonholes.

Knit 1 row. Cast off *loosely*.

Back Leg Opening Band

Work as for Front Leg Opening Band, omitting buttonholes. Sew on buttons. Press seams.

A pocket full of posies

With flowers embroidered on the sleeves and colours going every which way, your little girl will love this cardigan

MEASUREMENTS

This garment is designed to be a generous fit.

Size		A	B	C
Approx age	months	18	24	36
Fits underarm	cm	52.5	55	57.5
	ins	21	22	23
Garment measures	cm	58.5	62	65.5
Length	cm	35	37	39
Sleeve fits	cm	21	23	25
(or length desired)				

MATERIALS

Patons Bluebell 5 Ply or Patons 5 Ply Machinewash 50 g balls

Main colour (M)	3	3	4
1st contrast (C1)	2	2	3
2nd contrast (C2)	1	1	1
3rd contrast (C3)	small quantity for each size		
4th contrast (C4)	small quantity for each side		

ACCESSORIES

1 pair each 3.75 mm (no. 9) and 3.00 mm (no. 11) Milward knitting needles or sizes needed to give correct tension, 1 stitch holder, 7 buttons, 3.75 mm (no. 9) crochet hook for trimming.

TENSION

26.5 sts to 10 cm in width over stocking st, using 3.75 mm needles.
Please check your tension carefully. If less sts use smaller needles, if more sts use bigger needles.

Back

Using 3.00 mm needles and C1, cast on 82 (86,90) sts.
1st row K2, ★ P2, K2, rep from ★ to end.
2nd row P2, ★ K2, P2, rep from ★ to end.
Rep 1st and 2nd rows 6 times, dec once in centre of last row... 81 (85,89) sts, 14 rows rib in all.
Change to 3.75 mm needles.
1st row Using M, K4 (6,8), P1, K1, P1, ★ K7, P1, K1, P1, rep from ★ to last 4 (6,8) sts, K4 (6,8).
2nd row Using C2, knit all knit sts and purl all purl sts as they appear.
Rep 2nd row 6 times, using M instead of C2.
Rep 2nd row 6 times, using C1 instead of C2.
Last 14 rows form patt.
Cont in patt until work measures 20.5 (22,23.5) cm from beg, working last row on wrong side.

SHAPE RAGLAN ARMHOLES

Cast off 3 sts at beg of next 2 rows.
Keeping patt correct, dec at each end of next and foll 4th (4th,alt) rows until 71 (75,29) sts rem. **Sizes A and B only**, then in alt rows until 27 (29) sts rem. **All sizes**, work 1 row patt. Leave rem sts on stitch holder.

Left Front

Using 3.00 mm needles and C1, cast on 42 (42,46) sts.
Work 14 rows rib as for Back, dec 2 (0,2) sts evenly across last row... 40(42,44) sts.
Change to 3.75 mm needles.
1st row Using M, K4, (6,8), P1, K1, P1, ★ K7, P1, K1, P1, rep from ★ to last 3 sts, K3.
2nd row Using C2, knit all knit sts and purl all purl sts as they appear.
Cont in patt as for Back *as placed* in last 2 rows until work measures same as Back to armholes, ending with same row.

SHAPE RAGLAN

Keeping patt correct, cast off 3 sts at beg of next row.
Work 1 row patt.
Dec at beg of next and foll 4th (4th,alt) rows until 35 (37,22) sts rem. **Sizes A and B only**, then in alt rows until 20 (22) sts rem. **All sizes:**

SHAPE NECK

Cast off 6 sts at beg of next row.
Dec at each end of next and alt rows until 4 sts rem, then at armhole edge only in alt rows until 2 sts rem.
Next row Patt 2, *turn*, work 2 tog.
Fasten off.

Right Front

Work to correspond with Left Front, placing patt thus:
1st row Using M, K3, ★ P1, K1, P1, K7, rep from ★ to last 7 (9,11) sts, P1, K1, P1, K4 (6,8).

Sleeves

Using 3.00 mm needles and M, cast on 42 sts.
Work 14 rows rib as for Back, inc 3

73

(5,7) sts evenly across last row... 45 (47,49) sts

Change to 3.75 mm needles.

Work 4 rows stocking st.

5th row K2, "M1", knit to last 2 sts, "M1", K2.

Cont in stocking st, inc (as before) at each end of foll 8th (8th,10th) rows until there are 59 (61,63) sts.

Cont without shaping until work measures 21 (23,25) cm (or length desired) from beg, ending with a purl row.

SHAPE RAGLAN

Cast off 3 sts at beg of next 2 rows.

Dec at each end of next and foll 4th rows until 47 (49,51) sts rem, then in alt rows until 7 sts rem. Work 1 row. Cast off.

Neckband

Using backstitch, join raglan seams, noting that tops of Sleeves form part of neckline. With right side facing, using 3.00 mm needles and C1, knit up 82 (86,86) sts evenly around neck, incl sts from stitch holder.

Work 19 rows rib as for Back, beg with a 2nd row. Cast off *loosely* in rib.

Right Front Band

Fold Neckband in half onto wrong side and slipstitch in position. With right side facing, using 3.00 mm needles and C1, knit up 94 (106,106) sts evenly along right front edge, working through both thicknesses of Neckband.

Work 3 rows rib as for Back, beg with a 2nd row.

4th row Rib 4, ★ cast off 2 sts, rib 12 (14, 14), rep from ★ to last 6 sts, cast off 2 sts, rib 4.

5th row Rib 4, ★ *turn*, cast on 2 sts, *turn*, rib 12 (14,14), rep from ★ to last 4 sts, *turn*, cast on 2 sts, *turn*, rib 4... 7 buttonholes.

Work 4 rows rib. Cast off *loosely* in rib.

Left Front Band

Work as for Right Front Band, omitting buttonholes.

Make up

Using contrast colours as illustrated, work Crochet Chain Stripes up each purl rib on fronts and back as follows — holding yarn at back of work and using hook, draw a loop through to right side. Insert hook through stitch 2 rows above and draw another loop through, then through loop on hook (see diagram right). Using Knitting Stitch (see page 40), embroider elbow patch on sleeves from graph below. With a slightly damp cloth and warm iron, press lightly. Using backstitch, join side and sleeve seams. Sew on buttons. Press seams.

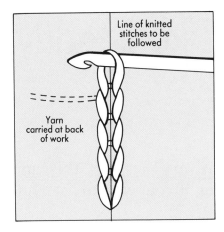

Key for Knitting Stitch embroidery
⊠ C1   ◙ C3   ⊡ C4

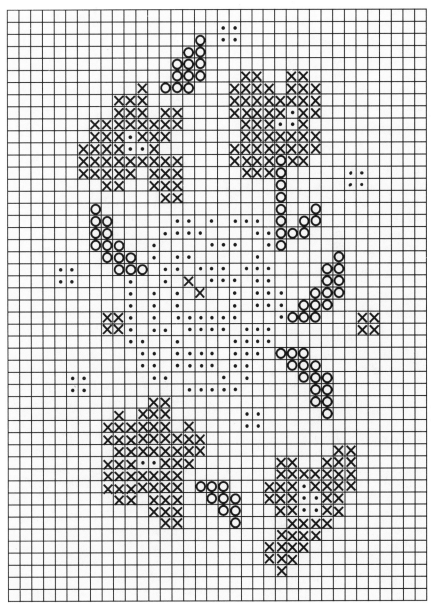

Like a teddy bear

BEGINNER

A very easy knit, this jumper can be done in one shade or, if you want to have fun with colours, in stripes

MEASUREMENTS
This garment is designed to be a generous fit.

Size		A	B	C
Approx age	months	18	24	36
Fits underarm	cm	52.5	55	57.5
	ins	21	22	23
Garment measures	cm	57.5	61	64.5
Length	cm	33	35	37
Sleeve fits	cm	21	23	25
(or length desired)				

MATERIALS
Patons Bluebell 5 Ply or Patons 5 Ply Machinewash 50 g balls

JUMPER WITH STRIPES
Main colour (M)	3	4	5
1st contrast (C1)	small quantity for each size		
2nd contrast (C2)	small quantity for each size		
3rd contrast (C3)	small quantity for each size		
4th contrast (C4)	small quantity for each size		

JUMPER WITHOUT STRIPES
	3	4	5

ACCESSORIES
1 pair each 3.75 mm (no. 9) and 3.00 mm (no. 11) Milward knitting needles or sizes needed to give correct tension, 3 stitch holders, 3 buttons.

TENSION
26.5 sts to 10 cm in width over stocking st, using 3.75 mm needles.
Please check your tension carefully. If less sts use smaller needles, if more sts use bigger needles.

Jumper with stripes
Back
Using 3.00 mm needles and M, cast on 78 (82,86) sts.
1st row K2, ★ P2, K2, rep from ★ to end.
2nd row P2, ★ K2, P2, rep from ★ to end.
Rep 1st and 2nd rows 6 times, inc once in centre of last row... 79 (83,87) sts.

Change to 3.75 mm needles.
Work in stocking st stripes of 8 rows M, 2 rows C1, 8 rows M, 2 rows C2, 8 rows M, 2 rows C3, 8 rows M, then 2 rows C4 throughout until work measures 19.5 (21,22.5) cm from beg, ending with a purl row.
Tie a coloured thread at each end of last row to mark beg of armholes as there is no armhole shaping. ★★
Work a further 12 (14,16) rows stripes.

DIVIDE FOR BACK OPENING
1st row K42 (44,46), *turn* and cont on these sts.
2nd row K5, purl to end.
3rd row Knit.
Rep 2nd and 3rd rows 4 times, then 2nd row once.
13th row Knit to last 3 sts, y fwd, K2 tog (buttonhole), K1.
Keeping garter st edge correct, work a further 15 rows.
Rep 13th row once.
Work 3 rows.

SHAPE SHOULDER
Keeping garter st edge and stripes correct, cast off 7 sts at beg of next and alt rows 3 times in all, then 5 (6,8) sts at beg of foll alt row.
Work 1 row. Leave rem 16 (17,17) sts on a stitch holder.
Join yarn to rem sts, cast on 5 sts for garter st underlap and work to correspond with other side, omitting buttonholes.

Front
Work as for Back to ★★.
Work a further 26 (26,28) rows stripes.

SHAPE NECK
Next row K34 (36,38), *turn* and cont on these sts.
Keeping stripes correct, dec at neck edge in alt rows until 26 (27,29) sts rem.
Work 1 row.

SHAPE SHOULDER

Cast off 7 sts at beg of next and alt rows 3 times in all.

Work 1 row. Cast off.

Slip next 11 sts onto a stitch holder and leave. Join yarn to rem sts and work other side to correspond.

Sleeves

Using 3.00 mm needles and M, cast on 38 (38,42) sts.

Work 14 rows rib as for Back, inc 9 sts evenly across last row... 47 (47,51) sts.

Change to 3.75 mm needles.

Work 4 rows stocking st.

5th row K2, "M1", knit to last 2 sts, "M1", K2.

Cont in stocking st, inc (as before) at each end of foll 4th rows until there are 65 (63,59) sts, then in foll 6th row/s until there are 67 (69,71) sts.

Cont without shaping until work measures 19 (21,23) cm (or 2 cm less than length desired to allow for loose fit) from beg, ending with a purl row.

Cast off 9 sts at beg of next 6 rows.

Cast off rem sts.

Neckband

Using backstitch, join shoulder seams. With right side facing, using 3.00 mm needles and M, knit up 96 (100,100) sts evenly around neck, incl sts from stitch holders.

Keeping garter st border correct, work 8 rows rib as for Back, beg with a 2nd row and working a buttonhole (as before) in 4th row... 3 buttonholes.

Cast off *loosely* in rib.

Make up

With a slightly damp cloth and warm iron, press lightly. Using backstitch, join sleeve and side seams to coloured threads. Sew in sleeves. Sew underlap in position. Sew on buttons. Press seams.

Jumper without stripes

Work as for Jumper with stripes, working in one colour only.

Two for joy

Knitted in easy-care Machinewash, the impact of this cardigan and jumper comes from cable stitches, picture knitting and the clever use of colour

MEASUREMENTS
This garment is designed to be a generous fit.

Size		A	B	C
Approx age	months	18	24	36
Fits underarm	cm	52.5	55	57.5
	ins	21	22	23
Garment measures	cm	60.5	63	67.5
Length	cm	36	38	40
Sleeve fits	cm	19	21	23
(or length desired)				

MATERIALS
Patons 5 Ply Machinewash or Patons Bluebell 5 Ply 50 g balls

JUMPER
Main colour (M)	2	3	4
1st contrast (C1)	1	1	2
2nd contrast (C2)	1	1	1
3rd contrast (C3)	1	1	1

CARDIGAN
Main colour (M)	3	4	5
1st contrast (C1)	1	1	1
2nd contrast (C2)	small quantity for each size		
3rd contrast (C3)	small quantity for each size		

ACCESSORIES
1 pair each 3.75 mm (no. 9) and 3.00 mm (no. 11) Milward knitting needles or sizes needed to give correct tension, 1 cable needle, 2 stitch holders for Jumper, 6 buttons for Cardigan.

SPECIAL ABBREVIATIONS
"Cable" = slip next 4 sts onto cable needle and leave at back of work, K4, then K4 from cable needle.

TENSION
26.5 sts and 35 rows to 10 cm over stocking st, using 3.75 mm needles.
Please check your tension carefully. If less sts use smaller needles, if more sts use bigger needles.

Jumper
Back
Using 3.00 mm needles and M, cast on 81 (85,91) sts.

1st row K2, ★ P1, K1, rep from ★ to last st, K1.

2nd row K1, ★ P1, K1, rep from ★ to end.

Rep 1st and 3rd rows 5 times... 12 rows rib in all.

Change to 3.75 mm needles.

Work 2 (4,10) rows stocking st.

Note When changing colours in the middle of a row, twist the colour to be used (on wrong side) underneath and to the right of the colour just used (see diagram on page 81). Wind colours into smaller balls where necessary.

BEG PATT

1st row K8 (10,13)M, K2C3, K19M, K2C2, K19M, K2C1, K19M, K2C2, K8 (10,13)M.

2nd row P7 (9,12)M, P4C2, P17M, P4C1, P17M, P4C2, P17M, P4C3, P7 (9,12)M.

3rd row K6 (8,11)M, K6C3, K15M, K6C2, K15M, K6C1, K15M, K6C2, K6 (8,11)M.

4th Row P5 (7,10)M, P8C2, P13M, P8C1, P13M, P8C2, P13M, P8C3, P5 (7,10)M.

5th row K4 (6,9)M, K10C3, K11M, K10C2, K11M, K10C1, K11M, K10C2, K4 (6,9)M.

6th row P3 (5,8)M, P12C2, P9M, P12C1, P9M, P12C2, P9M, P12C3, P3 (5,8)M.

7th row K2 (4,7)M, K14C3, K7M, K14C2, K7M, K14C1, K7M, K14C2, K2 (4,7)M.

8th row P1 (3,6)M, P16C2, P5M, P16C1, P5M, P16C2, P5M, P16C3, P1 (3,6)M.

9th row Using M, knit.

10th row Using M, purl.

11th row Using C1, K4 (6,9), ★ P2, K2, inc in each of next 2 sts, K2, P2, K11, rep from ★ twice, P2, K2, inc in each of next 2 sts, K2, P2, K4 (6,9)... 89 (93,99) sts.

12th and 14th rows P4 (6,9), ★ K2, P8, K2, P11, rep from ★ twice, K2, P8, K2, P4 (6,9).

13th row K4 (6,9), ★ P2, K8, P2, K11, rep from ★ twice, P2, K8, P2, K4 (6,9).

15th row K4 (6,9), ★ P2, "Cable", P2, K11, rep from ★ twice, P2, "Cable", P2, K4 (6,9).

Rep 12th and 13th rows 4 times, then 12th row once.

25th row As 15th row.

Rep 12th and 13th rows twice.

30th row P4 (6,9), ★ K2, P2, (P2 tog) twice, P2, K2, P11, rep from ★ twice, K2, P2, (P2 tog) twice, K2, P4 (6,9)... 81 (85,91) sts.

31st and 32nd rows As 9th and 10th rows.

33rd row K1 (3,6)M, K16C1, K5M, K16C3, K5M, K16C2, K5M, K16C1, K1 (3,6)M.

34th row P2 (4,7)M, P14C1, P7M, P14C2, P7M, P14C3, P7M, P14C1, P2 (4,7)M.

35th row K3 (5,8)M, K12C1, K9M, K12C3, K9M, K12C2, K9M, K12C1, K3 (5,8)M.

36th row P4 (6,9)M, P10C1, P11M, P10C2, P11M, P10C3, P11M, P10C1, P4 (6,9)M.

37th row K5 (7,10)M, K8C1, K13M, K8C3, K13M, K8C2, K13M, K8C1, K5 (7,10)M.

38th row P6 (8,11)M, P6C1, P15M, P6C2, P15M, P6C3, P15M, P6C1, P6 (8,11)M.

39th row K7 (9,12)M, K4C1, K17M, K4C3, K17M, K4C2, K17M, K4C1, K7 (9,12)M.

40th row P8 (10,13)M, P2C1, P19M, P2C2, P19M, P2C3, P19M, P2C1, P8 (10,13)M.

Last 40 rows form patt.

Using M, work 10 rows stocking st.

Rep rows 1 to 40 incl once. ★★

Using M for rem, work 18 (22,24) rows stocking st.

SHAPE SHOULDERS

Cast off 7 (7,8) sts at beg of next 6 rows, then 6 (7,7) sts at beg of foll 2 rows. Leave rem 27 (29,29) sts on a stitch holder.

Front

Work as for Back to ★★.

Using M for rem, work 0 (2,4) rows stocking st.

SHAPE NECK

Next row K35 (36,39), *turn*, and cont on these sts.

Dec at neck edge in alt rows until 27 (28,31) sts rem.

Work 1 (3,3) row/s stocking st.

SHAPE SHOULDER

Cast off 7 (7,8) sts at beg of next and alt rows 3 times in all.

Work 1 row. Cast off.

Slip next 11 (13,13) sts onto stitch holder and leave. Join yarn to rem sts and work other side to correspond.

Sleeves

Using 3.00 mm needles and M, cast on 41 (41,43) sts.

Work 12 rows rib as for Back, inc 8 sts evenly across last row... 49 (49,51) sts.

Change to 3.75 mm needles.

Work 4 rows stocking st.

5th row K2, "M1", knit to last 2 sts, "M1", K2.

Cont in stocking st, inc (as before) at each end of foll 4th row/s until there are 53 (57,55) sts, then in foll 6th rows until there are 65 (69,71) sts.

Cont without shaping until work measures 19 (21,23) cm (or length desired) from beg, ending with a purl row.

Cast off 9 (10,10) sts at beg of next 6 rows. Cast off rem sts.

Neckband

Using backstitch, join right shoulder seam. With right side facing, using 3.00 mm needles and M, knit up 81 (89,89) sts evenly around neck, incl sts from stitch holders.

Work 15 rows rib as for Back, beg with a 2nd row. Cast off *loosely* in rib.

Make up

With a slightly damp cloth and warm iron, press lightly, taking care not to flatten patt. Tie a coloured thread at side edges of back and front 22.5 (24,25.5) cm up from lower edge to mark position of armholes. Using backstitch, join left shoulder, sleeve and side seams to coloured threads. Sew in sleeves. Fold neckband in half onto wrong side and slipstitch in position. Press seams.

Cardigan

Back

Using 3.00 mm needles and M, cast on 81 (85,91) sts.

Work 12 rows rib as for Back of Jumper. Change to 3.75 mm needles.

Work 52 (54,60) rows stocking st.

Work rows 1 to 40 incl of patt as for Back of Jumper.

Using M for rem, work a further 18 (22,24) rows stocking st.

SHAPE SHOULDERS

Cast off 7 (7,8) sts at beg of next 6 rows, then 6 (7,7) sts at beg of foll 2 rows. Cast off rem 27 (29,29) sts.

Left Front

Using 3.00 mm needles and M, cast on 39 (41,45) sts.

Work 12 rows rib as for Back, inc 1 (1,0) st/s in centre of last row... 40 (42,45) sts.

Change to 3.75 mm needles.

Work 52 (54,60) rows stocking st.

Next row K8 (10,13)M, K2C3, K19M, K2C2, K9M.

Next row P8M, P4C2, P17M, P4C3, P7 (9,12)M.

Next row K6 (8,11)M, K6C3, K15M, K6C2, K7M.

Next row P6M, P8C2, P13M, P8C3, P5 (7,10)M.

Work a further 36 rows patt as for Back, *as placed* in last 4 rows.

Using M for rem, work 7 (9,11) rows stocking st.

SHAPE NECK

Cast off 6 sts at beg of next row.

Dec at neck edge in every row until 29 (31,34) sts rem, then in alt rows until 27 (28,31) sts rem. Work 1 row.

SHAPE SHOULDER

Cast off 7 (7,8) sts at beg of next and alt rows 3 times in all.

Work 1 row. Cast off.

Right Front

Work to correspond with Left Front, *placing* patt thus:

1st row K9M, K2C1, K19M, K2C2, K8 (10,13)M.

2nd row P7 (9,12)M, P4C2, P17M, P4C1, P8M.

3rd row K7M, K6C1, K15M, K6C2, K6 (8,11)M.

4th row P5 (7,10)M, P8C2, P13M, P8C1, P6M.

Sleeves

Work as for Sleeves of Jumper

Left Front Band

Using 3.00 mm needles and M, cast on 9 sts.

Work 122 (122,132) rows rib as for Back.

Leave sts on a safety pin. Break off yarn.

Right Front Band

Using 3.00 mm needles and M, cast on 9 sts.

Work 4 rows rib.

5th row Rib 4, cast off 2 sts, rib 3.

6th row Rib 3, *turn*, cast on 2 sts, *turn*, rib 4... buttonhole.

Work 22 (22,24) rows rib.

Rep last 24 (24,26) rows 3 times, then 5th and 6th rows once... 5 buttonholes.

Work 21 (21, 23) rows rib. Leave sts on needle, *do not* break off yarn.

Neckband

Using backstitch, join shoulder seams. Sew Front Bands in position. With right side facing, using 3.00 mm needle holding Right Front Band sts and M, knit up 79 (85,85) sts evenly around neck, then rib across Left Front Band sts... 97 (103,103) sts.

Work 7 rows rib as for Back, beg with a 2nd row and working a buttonhole (as before) in 2nd and 3rd rows.

Cast off 9 sts in rib at beg of next 2 rows.

Work 7 rows rib. Cast off in rib.

Make up

With a slightly damp cloth and warm iron, press lightly, taking care not to flatten patt. Tie a coloured thread at side edges of back and front 22.5 (24,25.5) cm up from lower edge to mark position of armholes. Using backstitch, join sleeve and side seams to coloured threads. Fold neckband in half onto wrong side and slipstitch in position. Sew on buttons. Press seams.

PICTURE KNITTING USING THE WINDING YARN METHOD

This is a simple method of knitting in motifs. It *must not* be interchanged with Fair Isle. When changing colours in the middle of a row, twist the colour to be used (on wrong side) underneath and to the right of the colour just used. As you begin each colour, give a gentle tug to even up loose stitches.

It is necessary to use a separate quantity of yarn for each section of colour. To minimise tangles, wind small amounts of yarn onto Susan Bates Yarn Bobs. Unwind only enough yarn to knit required stitches, keeping bob close to work.

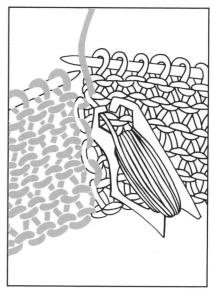

Friday's child

The tab front opening on this cable stitch jumper knitted in warm Bluebell makes dressing the squirmiest toddler easy

MEASUREMENTS
This garment is designed to be a generous fit.

Size		A	B	C
Approx age	months	18	24	36
Fits underarm	cm	52.5	55	57.5
	ins	21	22	23
Garment measures	cm	*60*	*63*	*66*
Length (approx)	cm	31	33	35
Sleeve fits	cm	21	23	25
(or length desired)				

MATERIALS

	A	B	C
Patons Bluebell 5 Ply 50 g balls	4	4	5

ACCESSORIES
1 pair each 3.75 mm (no. 9) and 3.00 mm (no. 11) Milward knitting needles or sizes needed to give correct tension, 1 cable needle, 2 buttons.

SPECIAL ABBREVIATIONS
"Cable" = slip next 2 sts onto cable needle and leave at back of work, K2, then K2 from cable needle.

TENSION
26.5 sts to 10 cm in width over stocking st, using 3.75 mm needles.
Please check your tension carefully. If less sts use smaller needles, if more sts use bigger needles.

Back
Using 3.00 mm needles, cast on 81 (85,89) sts.
1st row   K2, ★ P1, K1, rep from ★ to last st, K1.
2nd row   K1, ★ P1, K1, rep from ★ to end.
Rep 1st and 2nd rows 4 times, then 1st row once.
12th row   Rib 8 (4,6), ★ inc in next st, rib 4 (5,5), rep from ★ to last 8 (3,5) sts, inc in next st, rib 7 (2,4)... 95 (99,103) sts.
Change to 3.75 mm needles.
1st row   K3 (5,7), ★ P2, K4, P2, K7, P2, K1, P2, K7, rep from ★ to last 11 (13,15) sts, P2, K4, P2, K3, (5,7).
2nd row   Knit all knit sts and purl all purl sts as they appear.
Rep 1st and 2nd rows once.
5th row   K3 (5,7), ★ P2, "Cable", P2, K7, P2, K1, P2, K7, rep from ★ to last 11 (13,15) sts, P2, "Cable", P2, K3 (5,7).
6th row   As 2nd row.
Last 6 rows form patt.
Cont in patt until work measures approx 17.5 (19, 20.5) cm from beg, ending with a 6th patt row.
Tie a coloured thread at each end of last row to mark beg of armholes as there is no armhole shaping.
Work a further 12 rows patt. ★★

BEG YOKE PATT
1st row   K3, (5,7), ★ P2, K4, P2, K1, rep from ★ to last 11 (13,15) sts, P2, K4, P2, K3 (5,7).
2nd row   Knit all knit sts and purl all purl sts as they appear.
Rep 1st and 2nd rows once.
5th row   K3 (5,7), ★ P2, "Cable", P2, K1, rep from ★ to last 11 (13,15) sts, P2, "Cable", P2, K3 (5,7).
6th row   As 2nd row.
Last 6 rows form yoke patt for rem.
Work a further 26 (28,30) rows patt.

SHAPE SHOULDERS
Keeping patt correct, cast off 8 (8,9) sts at beg of next 6 rows, then 8 (9,8) sts at beg of foll 2 rows.
Cast off rem 31 (33,33) sts.

Front
Work as for Back to ★★.

DIVIDE FOR FRONT OPENING
Next row   K3 (5,7), ★ P2, K4, P2, K1 ★, rep from ★ to ★ 3 times, P2, K4, P1, cast off 3 sts, P1, K4, P2, K1, rep from ★ to ★ 3 times, P2, K4, P2, K3, (5,7).
Cont on last 46 (48,50) sts.
Work a further 19 (19,21) rows in yoke patt as for Back, *as placed* in last row.

SHAPE NECK

Cast off 7 (7,8) sts at beg of next row.
Keeping patt correct, dec at neck edge in every row until 35 (37,40) sts rem, then in alt rows until 32 (33,35) sts rem.
Work 2 rows patt.

SHAPE SHOULDER

Keeping patt correct, cast off 8 (8,9) sts at beg of next and alt rows 3 times in all. Work 1 row. Cast off.
Join yarn to rem sts and work other side to correspond.

Sleeves

Using 3.00 mm needles, cast on 41 (41,43) sts.
Work 12 rows rib as for Back, inc 8 (10,10) sts evenly across last row... 49 (51,53) sts.
Change to 3.75 mm needles.
Work 4 rows stocking st.
5th row K2, "M1", knit to last 2 sts, "M1", K2.
Cont in stocking st, inc (as before) at each end of foll 6th row/s until there are 59 (63,57) sts, then in foll 8th rows until there are 65 (69,71) sts.
Cont with shaping until work measures 21 (23,25) cm (or length desired) from beg, ending with a purl row.
Cast off 7 sts at beg of next 8 rows.
Cast off rem sts.

Neckband

Using backstitch, join shoulder seams.
With right side facing and using 3.00 mm needles, knit up 66 (72,78) sts evenly around neck.
Knit 4 rows garter st. Cast off.

Left Front Band

Using 3.00 mm needles, cast on 20 (22,22) sts.
Knit 2 rows garter st.
3rd row K4, cast off 2 sts, K8, (10,10), cast off 2 sts, K4.
4th row K4, *turn*, cast on 2 sts, *turn*, K8 (10,10), *turn*, cast on 2 sts, *turn*, K4... 2 buttonholes.
Knit 2 rows garter st. Cast off.

Continued on page 110

Mary, Mary

A profusion of flowers on a Fair Isle background creates a delightful addition to any little girl's wardrobe

MEASUREMENTS

This garment is designed to be a generous fit.

Size		A	B	C
Approx age	months	18	24	36
Fits underarm	cm	52.5	55	57.5
	ins	21	22	23
Garment measures	*cm*	*60.5*	*63*	*67.5*
Length	cm	36	38	40
Sleeve fits	cm	21	23	25

MATERIALS

Patons Bluebell 5 Ply 50 g balls

Main colour (M)	2	2	3
1st contrast (C1)	1	1	1
2nd contrast (C2)	1	1	2
3rd contrast (C3)	1	1	1

ACCESSORIES

1 pair each 3.75 mm (no. 9), 4.00 mm (no. 8) and 3.00 mm (no. 11) Milward knitting needles or sizes needed to give correct tension, 1 stitch holder, 6 buttons, tapestry yarn for embroidery.

TENSION

26.5 sts and 35 rows to 10 cm over stocking st, using 3.75 mm needles.
Please check your tension carefully. If less sts use smaller needles, if more sts use bigger needles.

Back

Using 3.00 mm needles and M, cast on 81 (85,91) sts.

1st row K2, ★ P1, K1, rep from ★ to last st, K1.

2nd row K1, ★ P1, K1, rep from ★ to end.

Rep 1st and 2nd rows 6 times... 14 rows rib in all.

Change to 3.75 mm needles and C1. Work 14 (18,24) rows stocking st.

★★ Change to 4.00 mm needles.

Note In Fair Isle patt, **do not weave** colours but carry colour not in use *loosely* across on wrong side. Always carry colours to ends of rows and always carry contrast above background colour.

BEG PATT

1st row K1 (3,0)C1, ★ K1C2, K5C1, rep from ★ to last 2 (4,1) st/s, K1C2, K1 (3,0)C1.

2nd and 4th rows Purl in same colours as previous row.

3rd row K0 (0,2)C2, K0 (2,3)C1, ★ K3C2, K3C1, rep from ★ to last 0 (2,5) sts, K0 (2,3)C1, K0 (0,2)C2.

5th row K4 (0,3)C2, ★ K1C1, K5C2, rep from ★ to last 5 (1,4) st/s, K1C1, K4 (0,3)C2.

6th row As 2nd row.

Change to 3.75 mm needles. ★★

Using C2, work 24 rows stocking st.

Rep from ★★ to ★★ using C2 in place of C1 and C3 in place of C2.

Using C3, work 14 rows stocking st.

Tie a coloured thread at each end of last row to mark beg of armholes as there is no armhole shaping.

Using C3, work a further 10 rows stocking st.

Using M for rem, work 34 (36,38) rows stocking st.

SHAPE SHOULDER

Cast off 7 sts at beg of next 6 rows, then 6 (7,10) sts at beg of foll 2 rows. Leave rem 27 (29,29) sts on stitch holder.

Left Front

Using 3.00 mm needles and M, cast on 39 (41,45) sts.

Work 14 rows rib as for Back, inc 1 (1,0) st/s in centre of last row... 40 (42,45) sts.

Change to 3.75 mm needles.

Using C1, work 14 (18,24) rows stocking st.

★★★ Change to 4.00 mm needles.

BEG PATT

1st row K1 (3,0)C1, ★ K1C2, K5C1, rep from ★ to last 3 sts, K1C2, K2C1.

2nd and 4th rows Purl in same colours as previous row.

3rd row K0 (0,2)C2, K0 (2,3)C1, ★ K3C2, K3C1, rep from ★ to last 4 sts, K3C2, K1C1.

5th row K4 (0,3)C2, ★ K1C1, K5C2, rep from ★ to end.

6th row As 2nd row.

Change to 3.75 mm needles. ★★★

Using C2, work 24 rows stocking st.

Rep from ★★★ to ★★★ using C2 in place of C1 and C3 in place of C2.

Using C3, work 14 rows stocking st.

Tie a coloured thread at end of last row to mark beg of armhole.

Using C3, work a further 10 rows stocking st.

Using M for rem, work 23 (23,25) rows stocking st.

SHAPE NECK

Cast off 6 sts at beg of next row.
Dec at neck edge in every row until 29 (31,34) sts rem, then in alt rows until 27 (28,31) sts rem. Work 1 row.

SHAPE SHOULDER

Cast off 7 sts at beg of next and alt rows 3 times in all.
Work 1 row. Cast off.

Right Front

Work to correspond with Left Front, *placing* patt thus:

1st row K2C1, K1C2, ★ K5C1, K1C2, rep from ★ to last 1 (3,0) st/s, K1 (3,0)C1.

2nd and 4th rows Purl in same colours as previous row.

3rd row K1C1, K3C2, ★ K3C1, K3C2, rep from ★ to last 0 (2,5) sts, K0 (2,3)C1, K0 (0,2)C2.

5th row ★ K5C2, K1C1, rep from ★ to last 4 (0,3) sts, K4 (0,3)C2.

6th row As 2nd row.

Sleeves

Using 3.00 mm needles and M, cast on 41 (41,43) sts.
Work 14 rows rib as for Back, inc 8

sts evenly across last row... 49 (49,51) sts.

Change to 3.75 mm needles and C1.
Work in stocking st, inc at each end of 5th and foll 6th rows until there are 53 (53,55) sts.
Work 5 rows stocking st.
Change to 4.00 mm needles.

Next row Inc in first st C1, K4 (4,5)C1, ★ K1C2, K5C1, rep from ★ to last 6 (6,7) sts, K1C2, K4 (4,5)C1, inc in last st C1.

Work a further 5 rows patt as for Back *as placed* in last row (noting inc).
Change to 3.75 mm needles.

Using C2, inc at each end of next and foll 6th rows until there are 63 (63,65) sts.
Work 5 rows stocking st.
Change to 4.00 mm needles.

Next row Inc in first st C2, K3 (3,4)C2, ★ K1C3, K5C2, rep from ★ to last 5 (5,6) sts, K1C3, K3 (3,4)C2, inc in last st C2.

Work a further 5 rows patt as for Back *as placed* in last row (noting inc).
Change to 3.75 mm needles.

Sizes B and C only, using C3, inc at each end of next row and foll 6th row. **All sizes**, 65 (69,71) sts.

Using C3 for rem, work 2 (3,9) rows stocking st.

Cast off 8 sts at beg of next 6 rows.
Cast off rem sts.

Left Front Band

Using 3.00 mm needles and M, cast on 9 sts.
Work 110 (110,120) rows rib as for Back.
Leave sts on a safety pin. Break off yarn.

Right Front Band

Using 3.00 mm needles and M, cast on 9 sts.
Work 4 rows rib as for Back.

5th row Rib 4, y fwd, K2 tog, rib 3... buttonhole.
Work 21 (21,23) rows rib.
Rep last 22 (22,24) rows 3 times, then 5th row once... 5 buttonholes.
Work 18 (18,20) rows rib. *Do not* break off yarn, leave sts on needle.

Continued on page 110

FRENCH KNOTS

Bring the thread out at the required position, hold the thread down with the left thumb and encircle the thread twice with the needle (A). Still holding the thread firmly, twist the needle back to the starting point and insert it close to where the thread first emerged. Pull thread through to the back and secure for a single French Knot, or pass on to the position of the next stitch (B).

CHAIN STITCH

Bring the thread out at the top of the line and hold it down with left thumb. Insert the needle where it last emerged and bring the point out a short distance away. Pull the thread through, keeping the working thread under the needle point.

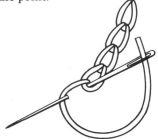

LAZY DAISY STITCH

Work in the same way as Chain Stitch (A), but fasten each loop at the foot with a small stitch (B). This stitch may be worked singly or in groups to form flower petals.

Miss Muffet

MEASUREMENTS

This garment is designed to be a generous fit.

Size		A	B	C
Approx age	months	18	24	36
Fits underarm	cm	52.5	55	57.5
	ins	21	22	23
Garment measures	cm	60.5	63	67.5
Length	cm	36	38	40
Sleeve fits	cm	21	23	25

MATERIALS

Patons Bluebell 5 Ply 50 g balls	5	5	6

ACCESSORIES

1 pair each 3.75 mm (no. 9) and 3.00 mm (no. 11) Milward knitting needles or sizes needed to give correct tension, 1 stitch holder, 6 buttons. For embroidery — Anchor or Semco stranded cotton in Blue Green and Rose Pink (Anchor shades 0850 and 076, Semco shades 920 and 859), 20 cm of 60 cm wide 10 count waste canvas, tapestry needle.

TENSION

26.5 sts to 10 cm in width over stocking st, using 3.75 mm needles.

Please check your tension carefully. If less sts use smaller needles, if more sts use bigger needles.

A line of waste canvas embroidered flowers on a classic stocking stitch design results in an enchanting cardigan for a little girl

Back

Using 3.00 mm needles, cast on 81 (85,91) sts.

1st row K2, ★ P1, K1, rep from ★ to last st, K1.

2nd row K1, ★ P1, K1, rep from ★ to end.

Rep 1st and 2nd rows 6 times... 14 rows rib in all.

Change to 3.75 mm needles.

Work in stocking st until work measures 22.5 (24,25.5) cm from beg, ending with a purl row.

Tie a coloured thread at each end of last row to mark beg of armholes as there is no armhole shaping. ★★

Work a further 44 (46,48) rows stocking st.

SHAPE SHOULDERS

Cast off 7 sts at beg of next 6 rows, then 6 (7,10) sts at beg of foll 2 rows.

Leave rem 27 (29,29) sts on stitch holder.

Left Front

Using 3.00 mm needles, cast on 39 (41,45) sts.

Work 14 rows rib as for Back, inc 1 (1,0) st/s in centre of last row... 40 (42,45) sts.

Change to 3.75 mm needles.

Work as for Back to ★★.

Work a further 33 (33,35) rows stocking st.

SHAPE NECK

Cast off 6 sts at beg of next row.

Dec at neck edge in every row until 29 (31,34) sts rem, then in alt rows until 27 (28,31) sts rem.

Work 1 row.

SHAPE SHOULDER

Cast off 7 sts at beg of next and alt rows 3 times in all. Work 1 row.

Cast off.

Right Front

Work to correspond with Left Front.

Sleeves

Using 3.00 mm needles, cast on 41 (41,43) sts.

Work 14 rows rib as for Back, inc 8 sts evenly across last row... 49 (49,51) sts.

Change to 3.75 mm needles.

Work 4 rows stocking st.

5th row K2, "M1", knit to last 2 sts, "M1", K2.

Cont in stocking st, inc (as before) at each end of foll 4th rows until there are 57 (63,59) sts, then in foll 6th rows until there are 65 (69,71) sts.

Cont without shaping until work measures 19 (21,23) cm (or 2 cm less than

length desired to allow for loose fit) from beg, ending with a purl row.

Cast off 8 sts at beg of next 6 rows.

Cast off rem sts.

Left Front Band

Using 3.00 mm needles, cast on 9 sts.

Work 110 (110,122) rows rib as for Back.

Leave sts on a safety pin. Break off yarn.

Right Front Band

Using 3.00 mm needles, cast on 9 sts.

Work 4 rows rib as for Back.

5th row Rib 4, y fwd, K2 tog, rib 3... buttonhole.

Work 21 (21,23) rows rib.

Rep last 22 (22,24) rows 3 times, then 5th row once... 5 buttonholes.

Work 18 (18,22) rows rib. *Do not* break off yarn, leave sts on needle.

Neckband

Using backstitch, join shoulder seams. Sew Front Bands in position. With right side facing and using 3.00 mm needle holding Right Front Band sts, knit up 69 (75,79) sts evenly around neck, incl sts from stitch holder, then rib across Left Front Band sts... 87 (93,97) sts.

Work 7 rows rib as for Back, beg with a 2nd row and working a buttonhole (as before) in 4th row.

Cast off 9 sts in rib at beg of next 2 rows.

Work 7 rows rib.

Cast off *loosely* in rib.

Key for Cross Stitch
☒ Rose Pink
☒ Blue Green

Make up

Cut waste canvas into 2 equal strips, then cut each strip in half. Tack each of these short pieces onto the right side of each sleeve just above the rib. For extra stability, you may care to attach some non-woven interfacing to the wrong side of the sleeve. Work the counted Cross Stitch (see graph below) using one length of thread and beg at the bottom of the green leaves. Centre one flower on the sleeve, then work as many flowers as will fit across the width of the sleeve. Work cardigan fronts in same manner. To remove canvas, dampen canvas with a water sprayer until it is soft and pliable. Remove tacking, then using tweezers remove all horizontal, then all vertical, threads one at a time. With a slightly damp cloth and warm iron, press lightly. Using backstitch, join sleeve and side seams to coloured threads. Sew in sleeves. Fold neckband in half onto wrong side and slipstitch in position. Sew on buttons. Press seams.

CROSS STITCH

Work one half of each Cross Stitch in a row, then return and complete the remaining half. Ensure the upper halves of all stitches lie in the same direction.

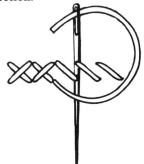

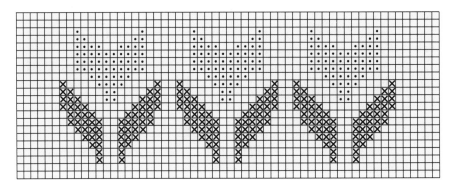

Queen of Hearts

Clever use of simple knit and purl stitches gives the chequered heart pattern on this Machinewash vest

MEASUREMENTS

This garment is designed to be a generous fit.

Size		A	B	C
Approx age	months	18	24	36
Fits underarm	cm	52.5	55	57.5
	ins	21	22	23
Garment measures	*cm*	*60*	*63*	*66*
Length	cm	31	33	36

MATERIALS

Patons 8 Ply Machinewash 50 g balls	3	4	4

ACCESSORIES

1 pair each 4.00 mm (no. 8) and 3.25 mm (no. 10) Milward knitting needles or sizes needed to give correct tension, 2 buttons.

TENSION

22.5 sts and 37 rows to 10 cm over patt, using 4.00 mm needles.
Please check your tension carefully. If less sts use smaller needles, if more sts use bigger needles.

Back and Front

Alike.
Using 3.25 mm needles, cast on 69 (71,73) sts.
1st row K2, ★ P1, K1, rep from ★ to last st, K1.
2nd row K1, ★ P1, K1, rep from ★ to end.
Rep 1st and 2nd rows 4 (4,5) times, inc once in centre of last row... 70 (72,74) sts, 10 (10,12) rows rib in all.
Change to 4.00 mm needles.

BEG PATT

Knit 4 rows garter st.
5th and alt rows Knit.
6th row P0 (1,2), ★ K2, P15, rep from ★ to last 2 (3,4) sts, K2, P0 (1, 2).
8th row P0 (1,2), ★ K2, P7, K1, P7, rep from ★ to last 2 (3,4) sts, K2, P0, (1,2).

10th row P0 (1,2), ★ K2, P6, K3, P6, rep from ★ to last 2 (3,4) sts, K2, P0 (1,2).
12th row P0 (1,2), ★ K2, P4, K7, P4, rep from ★ to last 2 (3,4) sts, K2, P0 (1,2).
14th row P0 (1,2), ★ K2, P3, K9, P3, rep from ★ to last 2 (3,4) sts, K2, P0, (1,2).
16th and 18th rows P0 (1,2), ★ K2, P2, K11, P2, rep from ★ to last 2 (3,4) sts, K2, P0 (1,2).
20th row P0 (1,2), ★ K2, P2, K5, P1, K5, P2, rep from ★ to last 2 (3,4) sts, K2, P0 (1,2).
22nd row P0 (1,2), ★ K2, P3, (K3, P3) twice, rep from ★ to last 2 (3,4) sts, K2, P0 (1,2).
24th row As 6th row.
Last 24 rows form patt.
Rep last 24 rows 3 (3,4) times.
Knit 5 (15,3) rows garter st. Cast off.

Make up

With a slightly damp cloth and warm iron, press lightly, taking care not to flatten patt. Using backstitch, join shoulder seams, leaving 18.5 (19,19.5) cm free in centre for neck. Tie a coloured thread at side edges of back and front 17.5 (19,21.5) cm up from lower edge to mark position of armholes. Join side seams to coloured threads. Make a buttonloop on each front shoulder and sew on buttons to correspond. Press seams.

Peter Piper

The coldest winter day will be no match for this cable patterned jumper knitted in extra warm Totem

MEASUREMENTS
This garment is designed to be a generous fit.

Size		A	B	C
Approx age	months	18	24	36
Fits underarm	cm	52.5	55	57.5
	ins	21	22	23
Garment measures	cm	60.5	63	67.5
Length	cm	36	38	40
Sleeve fits	cm	21	23	25

MATERIALS

	A	B	C
Patons Totem 8 Ply 50 g balls	6	7	8

ACCESSORIES
1 pair each 4.00 mm (no. 8) and 3.25 mm (no. 10) Milward knitting needles or sizes needed to give correct tension, 1 cable needle, 2 stitch holders.

SPECIAL ABBREVIATIONS
"Cable" = slip next 3 sts onto cable needle and leave at back of work, K3, then K3 from cable needle.

TENSION
24 sts to 10 cm in width over patt, using 4.00 mm needles.
Please check your tension carefully. If less sts use small needles, if more sts use bigger needles.

Back
Using 3.25 mm needles, cast on 75 (77,83) sts.
1st row K2, ★ P1, K1, rep from ★ to last st, K1.
2nd row K1, ★ P1, K1, rep from ★ to end.
Rep 1st and 2nd rows 5 times, dec (inc,inc) once in centre of last row... 74 (78,84) sts.
Change to 4.00 mm needles.
1st, 3rd and 5th rows Knit.
2nd, 4th and 6th rows K7 (9,12), ★ P6, K12, rep from ★ ending last rep with K7 (9,12) instead of K12.
7th row K7 (9,12), ★ "Cable", K12, rep from ★ ending last rep with K7 (9,12) instead of K12.
8th, 10th and 12th rows As 2nd row.
9th, 11th, 13th, 15th and 17th rows Knit.
14th, 16th and 18th rows K16 (18,3), ★ P6, K12, rep from ★ ending last rep with K16 (18,3) instead of K12.
19th row K16 (18,3), ★ "Cable", K12, rep from ★ ending last rep with K16 (18,3) instead of K12.
20th and 22nd rows As 14th row.
21st and 23rd rows Knit.
24th row As 14th row.
Last 24 rows form patt.
Cont in patt until work measures 22.5 (24,25.5) cm from beg, working last row on wrong side.
Tie a coloured thread at each end of last row to mark beg of armholes as there is no armhole shaping. ★★
Work a further 48 (50,52) rows patt.

SHAPE SHOULDERS
Keeping patt correct, cast off 6 (6,7) sts at beg of next 6 rows, then 6 (7,7) sts at beg of foll 2 rows.
Leave rem 26 (28,28) sts on a stitch holder.

Front
Work as for Back to ★★.
Work a further 28 (28,30) rows patt.

SHAPE NECK
Next row Patt 32 (34,37), *turn* and cont on these sts.
Keeping patt correct, dec at neck edge in alt rows until 24 (25,28) sts rem.
Work 3 rows patt.

SHAPE SHOULDER
Keeping patt correct, cast off 6 (6,7) sts at beg of next and alt rows 3 times in all. Work 1 row. Cast off.
Slip next 10 sts onto stitch holder and leave. Join yarn to rem sts and work other side to correspond.

Continued on page 110

Lucy Locket

The gay pattern on this fun outfit of matching skirt, jumper and bag is achieved with knitting stitch embroidery, Fair Isle and six fashion colours

MEASUREMENTS

The jumper is designed to be a generous fit.

Size		A	B	C
Approx age	months	18	24	36
JUMPER				
Fits underarm	cm	52.5	55	57.5
	ins	21	22	23
Garment measures	cm	56.5	60	62.5
Length	cm	24	26	28
Sleeve fits	cm	21	23	25
(or length desired)				
SKIRT				
Length	cm	24	26	29

MATERIALS

Patons Stonewash Cotton 8 Ply 50 g balls

JUMPER			
Main colour (M)	2	2	2
1st contrast (C1)	1	1	1
2nd contrast (C2)	1	1	1
3rd contrast (C3)	1	1	1
4th contrast (C4)	1	1	1
5th contrast (C5)	1	1	1
SKIRT			
Main colour (M)	2	2	3
1st contrast (C1)	1	1	1
2nd contrast (C2)	1	1	1
3rd contrast (C3)	1	1	1
4th contrast (C4)	1	1	1
5th contrast (C5)	1	1	1

BAG   small quantity of each colour

ACCESSORIES

1 pair each 4.00 mm (no. 8) and 4.50 mm (no. 7) Milward knitting needles or sizes needed to give correct tension, 2 stitch holders for Jumper, length of 1.5 cm elastic for Skirt, button and press stud for Bag.

TENSION

22 sts to 10 cm in width over stocking st, using 4.00 mm needles.
Please check your tension carefully. If less sts use smaller needles, if more sts use bigger needles.

Jumper

Back

Using 4.00 mm needles and C1, cast on 65 (67,69) sts.
Work 7 rows stocking st.
Knit 1 row (ridge).
Change to 4.50 mm needles.
Note In Fair Isle patt, **do not weave** colours but carry colour not in use *loosely* across on wrong side. It is important, however, that no colour should be carried across more than 7 sts, and where this is necessary it should be woven under and over colour in use at centre st. Always carry colours to ends of rows and always carry background colour above contrasts.
1st row K7 (8,9)C1, ★ K1C2, K9C1, rep from ★ to last 8 (9,10) sts, K1C2, K7 (8,9)C1.
2nd row P0 (0,1)C2, P6, (7,7)C1, ★ P3C2, P7C1, rep from ★ to last 9 (0,1) st/s, P3 (0,1)C2, P6 (0,0)C1.
3rd row K0 (1,2)C2, ★ K5C1, K5C2, rep from ★ to last 5 (6,7) sts, K5C1, K0 (1,2)C2.
4th row P1 (2,3)C2, ★ P3C1, P7C2, rep from ★ to last 4 (5,6) sts, P3C1, P1 (2,3)C2.
5th row K2 (3,4)C2, ★ K1C1, K9C2, rep from ★ to last 3 (4,5) sts, K1C1, K2 (3,4)C2.
6th row Using C2, purl.
7th row Using C2, knit.
8th and 9th rows As 6th and 7th rows, using C3 in place of C2.
10th and 12th rows P0 (0,1)C3, P1, (2,2)C4, ★ P3C3, P2C4, rep from ★ to last 4 (5,6) sts, P3C3, P1 (2,2)C4, P0 (0,1)C3.
11th row Knit in same colours as previous row.
13th row As 7th row, using C4 in place of C2.
14th row As 6th row, using C4 in place of C2.

Key for Knitting Stitch embroidery

☐ Main colour

⊡ Contrast

15th and 16th rows As 13th and 14th rows, using C1 in place of C4.

17th to 21st rows As rows 8 to 12, using C5 instead of C3 and M instead of C4 (working knit for purl and purl for knit).

Change to 4.00 mm needles.

Using M for rem, work in stocking st (beg with a purl row) until work measures 10.5 (12,13.5) cm from garter ridge, ending with a purl row.

Tie a coloured thread at each end of last row to mark beg of armholes as there is no armhole shaping. ★★

Work a further 36 (38,38) rows stocking st.

SHAPE SHOULDERS

Cast off 5 sts at beg of next 6 rows, then 5 (5,6) sts at beg of foll 2 rows. Leave rem 25 (27,27) sts on a stitch holder.

Front

Work as for Back to ★★.

Work a further 22 rows stocking st.

SHAPE NECK

Next row K26 (27,28), *turn* and cont on these sts.

Dec at neck edge in alt rows until 20 (20,21) sts rem.

Work 1 row.

SHAPE SHOULDER

Cast off 5 sts at beg of next and alt rows 3 times in all.

Work 1 row. Cast off.

Slip next 13 sts onto stitch holder and leave. Join yarn to rem sts and work other side to correspond.

Sleeves

Using 4.00 mm needles and C3, cast on 39 (41,43) sts.

Work 7 rows stocking st.
Knit 1 row (ridge).
Change to 4.50 mm needles.

1st row K4 (5,6)C2, ★ K1C3, K9C2, rep from ★ ending last rep with K4 (5,6)C2 instead of K9C2.

2nd row P3 (4,5)C2, ★ P3C3, P7C2, rep from ★ ending last rep with P3 (4,5)C2 instead of P7C2.

(Sleeve is worked in patt as for Back *as placed* in last 2 rows, using C2 instead of C1, C3 instead of C2, C1 instead of C3, C5 instead of C4 and C4 instead of C5.)

Work a further 2 rows patt.

Keeping patt correct, inc at each end of next and foll 4th (6th,6th) rows until there are 49 (47,49) sts.

Work a further 0 (4,4) rows patt as for Back.

Change to 4.00 mm needles.

Using M for rem, inc at each end of foll 6th rows from previous inc until there are 55 (57,59) sts.

Cont without shaping until work measures 19 (21,23) cm (or 2 cm less than length desired to allow for loose fit) from garter ridge, working last row on wrong side.

Cast off 8 sts at beg of next 6 rows.
Cast off rem sts.

Neckband

Using backstitch, join right shoulder seam. With right side facing, using 4.00 mm needles and C5, knit up 73 (79,79) sts evenly around neck, incl sts from stitch holders.

1st row Using C5, purl.

2nd row K1 (4,4)C5, ★ K1C3, K9C5, rep from ★ ending last rep with K1 (4,4)C5 instead of K9C5.

3rd row P0 (3,3)C5, ★ P3C3, P7C5, rep from ★ to last 3 (6,6) sts, P3C3, P0 (3,3)C5.

4th row K0 (2,2)C5, K4 (5,5)C3, ★ K5C5, K5C3, rep from ★ to last 9 (12,12) sts, K5C5, K4 (5,5)C3, K0 (2,2)C5.

5th row P0 (1,1)C5, P5 (7,7)C3, ★ P3C5, P7C3, rep from ★ to last 8 (11,11) sts, P3C5, P5 (7,7)C3, P0 (1,1)C5.

6th row K6 (9,9)C3, ★ K1C5, K9C3, rep from ★ ending last rep with K6 (9,9)C3 instead of K9C3.

Using C3 for rem, work 2 rows stocking st.

Next row Knit (ridge).

Work 8 rows stocking st, beg with a knit row. Cast off.

Make up

With a slightly damp cloth and warm iron, press lightly. Using Knitting Stitch (see page 40), embroider contrasting colour spots from graph (see page 94) at random as illustrated. Using backstitch, join left shoulder, sleeve and side seams to coloured threads. Sew in sleeves. Fold neckband, lower edge and sleeves to inside at ridge and slipstitch in position.

Skirt

Make 2.

Using 4.00 mm needles and C3, cast on 117 (123,129) sts.

Work 7 rows stocking st.

Knit 1 row (ridge).

Change to 4.50 mm needles.

1st row K3 (6,9)C3, ★ K1C5, K9C3, rep from ★ ending last rep with K3 (6,9)C3 instead of K9C3.

2nd row P0 (0,1)C5, P2 (5,7)C3, ★ P3C5, P7C3, rep from ★ to last 5 (8,1) st/s, P3 (3,1)C5, P2 (5,0)C3.

Cont in patt as for Back of Jumper, *as placed* in last 2 rows, until row 7 has been completed.

Change to 4.00 mm needles.

Using M, work 23 (25,31) rows stocking st.

★★★ Using C4, work 2 rows stocking st.

Using C1, work 2 rows stocking st.

Change to 4.50 mm needles.

Next row K0 (3,1)C1, ★ K2C2, K3C1, rep from ★ to last 2 (0,3) sts, K2 (0,2)C2, K0 (0,1)C1.

Work 2 rows in same colours.

Change to 4.00 mm needles.

Using C2, work 2 rows stocking st (beg with a purl row).

Using M for rem, **Next row** K3 (2,1), ★ K2 tog, K2, rep from ★ to last 2 (1,0) st/s, K2 (1,0)... 89 (93,97) sts.

1st row K1, ★ P1, K1, rep from ★ to end.

2nd row K2, ★ P1, K1, rep from ★ to last st, K1.

Rep 1st and 2nd rows 8 (10,11) times.

Next row P9 (8,10), ★ P2 tog, P1, rep from ★ to last 8 (7,9) sts, P8 (7,9)... 65 (67, 71) sts.

Work 12 rows stocking st. Cast off.

Make up

With a slightly damp cloth and warm iron, press lightly. Using Knitting Stitch (see page 40), embroider contrasting colour spots from graph (see page 94) at random as illustrated. Using backstitch, join side seams. Fold stocking st at waistband in half onto wrong side and slipstitch in position, leaving opening for elastic. Thread elastic through casing, slipstitch opening in position. Fold lower edge to inside at garter ridge and slipstitch in position. Press seams.

Bag

Using 4.00 mm needles and M, cast on 29 sts.

Work in stripes of 2 rows M, 8 rows C5, 2 rows C1, 8 rows C4, 2 rows C3.

Work rows 1 to 5 incl as for **Size C** for Back of Jumper.

Work 6 rows C2.

Rep rows 5 to 1 incl in reverse order, working purl for knit and knit for purl.

Work in stripes of 2 rows C3, 8 rows C4, 2 rows C1, 8 rows C5, and 2 rows M.

Using M for rem, knit in garter st, dec at each end of alt rows until 15 sts rem, then in every row until 5 sts rem. Cast off.

Make up

With a slightly damp cloth and warm iron, press lightly. Using backstitch, join side seams. Sew button in position (as illustrated) on right side of flap, then press stud on wrong side to correspond. Using 4 strands of M 180 cm long, make a twisted cord (see page 66) and sew in position as illustrated.

Rep from ★★★ once (working purl for knit and knit for purl), using C5 in place of C4, C3 in place of C1, C4 in place of C2 and C5 for last stripe.

Jack-a-Dandy

A simple cardigan made eye-catching through the use of strong bands of colour and the addition of a pocket

MEASUREMENTS
This garment is designed to be a generous fit.

Size		A	B	C
Approx age	months	18	24	36
Fits underarm	cm	52.5	55	57.5
	ins	21	22	23
Garment measures	cm	60.5	63	67.5
Length	cm	36	38	40
Sleeve fits	cm	21	23	25
(or length desired)				

MATERIALS
Patons Totem 8 Ply or Patons 8 Ply Machinewash 50 g balls

	A	B	C
1st colour (C1)	2	2	3
2nd colour (C2)	2	2	2
3rd colour (C3)	1	2	2

ACCESSORIES
1 pair each 4.00 mm (no. 8) and 3.25 mm (no. 10) Milward knitting needles or sizes needed to give correct tension, 1 stitch holder, 5 buttons.

TENSION
22.5 sts to 10 cm in width over stocking st, using 4.00 mm needles.
Please check your tension carefully. If less sts use smaller needles, if more sts use bigger needles.

Back
Using 3.25 mm needles and C3, cast on 69 (71,75) sts.
1st row K2, ★ P1, K1, rep from ★ to last st, K1.
2nd row K1, ★ P1, K1, rep from ★ to end.
Rep 1st and 2nd rows 5 times... 12 rows rib in all.
Change to 4.00 mm needles and C1.
Work 36 (38,40) rows stocking st.
Using C2 for rem, work in stocking st until work measures 22.5 (24,25.5) cm from beg, ending with a purl row.
Tie a coloured thread at each end of last row to mark beg of armholes as there is no armhole shaping.

Work a further 36 (38,38) rows stocking st.

SHAPE SHOULDERS
Cast off 6 sts at beg of next 6 rows, then 5 (5,7) sts at beg of foll 2 rows.
Cast off rem 23 (25,25) sts.

Pocket Lining
Make 1.
Using 4.00 mm needles and C1, cast on 15 (17,19) sts.
Work 22 rows stocking st. Leave sts on a stitch holder.

Left Front
Using 3.25 mm needles and C3, cast

on 34 (35,37) sts.
Work 12 rows rib as for Back.
Change to 4.00 mm needles and C1.
Work 22 rows stocking st.

PLACE POCKET
Next row K9, with right side facing knit across pocket lining sts, slip next 15 (17,19) sts onto stitch holder and leave for pocket top, K10 (9,9).
Work a further 13 (15,17) rows stocking st.
Using C2 for rem work in stocking st until work measures same as Back to coloured threads, ending with a purl row.
Tie a coloured thread at end of last row to mark beg of armhole.

SHAPE FRONT SLOPE
Dec at end of next and alt rows until 29 (30,32) sts rem, then in foll 4th rows until 23 (23,25) sts rem.
Work 3 (1,1) row/s.

SHAPE SHOULDER
Cast off 6 sts at beg of next and alt rows 3 times in all.
Work 1 row. Cast off.

Right Front
Work to correspond with Left Front, omitting pocket.

Sleeves
Using 3.25 mm needles and C3, cast on 33 (35,35) sts.
Work 12 rows rib as for Back, inc 8 sts evenly across last row... 41 (43,43) sts.
Change to 4.00 mm needles and C1.
Work 4 rows stocking st.
5th row K2, "M1", knit to last 2 sts, "M1", K2.
Cont in stocking st, inc (as before) at each end of foll 4th (6th,6th) rows until there are 55 (57,59) sts.
Cont without shaping until work measures 19 (21,23) cm (or 2 cm less than length desired) from beg, ending with a purl row.
Cast off 6 sts at beg of next 6 rows.
Cast off rem sts.

Front Band
Using backstitch, join shoulder seams.

Using 3.25 mm needles and C3, cast on 9 sts.
Work 4 rows rib as for Back.

FOR BOY

5th row Rib 3, cast off 2 sts, rib 4.
6th row Rib 4, *turn*, cast on 2 sts, *turn*, rib 3.

FOR GIRL

5th row Rib 4, cast off 2 sts, rib 3.
6th row Rib 3, *turn*, cast on 2 sts, *turn*, rib 4.

FOR BOY OR GIRL

Work 12 (14,14) rows rib.
Rep last 14 (16,16) rows 3 times, then 5th and 6th rows once... 5 buttonholes.
Cont without further buttonholes until Band is length required to fit (slightly stretched) along Fronts and across Back neck. Cast off in rib.

Pocket Top

Slip sts from stitch holder onto a 3.25 mm needle so that right side will be facing.
Using C3, knit 1 row, then work 6 rows rib as for Back, beg with a 2nd row. Cast off *loosely* in rib.

Make up

With a slightly damp cloth and warm iron, press lightly. Using backstitch, join sleeve and side seams to coloured threads. Sew in sleeves. Sew front band in position. Slipstitch pocket lining and ends of pocket top in position. Sew on buttons. Press seams.

MEASUREMENTS

The jumper and cardigan are designed to be a generous fit.

Size		A	B	C
Approx age	months	18	24	36
Fits underarm	cm	52.5	55	57.5
	ins	21	22	23

JUMPER

		A	B	C
Jumper measures	cm	58.5	62	65.5
Length	cm	34	36	38
Sleeve fits	cm	21	23	25

CARDIGAN

		A	B	C
Cardigan measures	cm	60.5	64	67.5
Length	cm	36	38	40
Sleeve fits	cm	21	23	25

HAT

		A	B	C
Fits head	cm	51	51	52

MATERIALS

Patons Bluebell 5 Ply or Patons 5 Ply Machinewash 50 g balls

JUMPER

	A	B	C
1st colour (C1)	1	1	2
2nd colour (C2)	1	1	2
3rd colour (C3)	1	1	2
4th colour (C4)	1	1	1

CARDIGAN

	A	B	C
1st colour (C1)	1	2	2
2nd colour (C2)	1	1	2
3rd colour (C3)	1	2	2
4th colour (C4)	1	1	1

HAT

	A	B	C
1st colour (C1)	1	1	1
2nd colour (C2)	1	1	1
4th colour (C4)	1	1	1

SCARF

	A	B	C
3rd colour (C3)	2	2	2

ACCESSORIES

1 pair each 3.75 mm (no. 9), 4.00 mm (no. 8) and 3.00 mm (no. 11) Milward knitting needles or sizes needed to give correct tension, 1 stitch holder for Jumper, 5 buttons for Cardigan, crochet hook for fringe on Scarf.

TENSION

26.5 sts and 35 rows to 10 cm over stocking st, using 3.75 mm needles

Please check your tension carefully. If less sts use smaller needles, if more sts use bigger needles.

Pease porridge hot

Use warm, bright colours and a striking
Fair Isle design to wrap up against
the winter cold

Jumper

Back

Using 3.00 mm needles and C4, cast on 79 (85,89) sts.

1st row K2, ★ P1, K1, rep from ★ to last st, K1.

2nd row K1, ★ P1, K1, rep from ★ to end.

Rep 1st and 2nd rows 6 times... 14 rows rib in all.

Change to 3.75 mm needles.

Work 4 rows stocking st.

Change to 4.00 mm needles.

Note In Fair Isle patt, **do not weave** colours but carry colour not in use *loosely* across on wrong side. It is important, however, that no colour should be carried across more than 7 sts, and where this is necessary it should be woven under and over colour in use at centre st. Always carry colours to ends of rows and always carry C1 above C4.

Work rows 1 to 12 incl from Graph A (see page 104).

Change to 3.75 mm needles.

Using C1, work in stocking st until work measures 20.5 (22,23.5) cm from beg, ending with a purl row.

Tie a coloured thread at each end of last row to mark beg of armholes as there is no armhole shaping. ★★

Using C2 for rem, work 44 (46,48) rows stocking st.

SHAPE SHOULDERS

Cast off 7 sts at beg of next 4 rows, then 6 (7,8) sts at beg of foll 4 rows. Cast off rem 27 (29,29) sts.

Front

Work as for Back to ★★.

Using C2 for rem, work 32 (32,34) rows stocking st.

SHAPE NECK

Next row K33 (36,38), *turn* and cont on these sts.

Dec at neck edge in every row until 29 (32,34) st rem, then in alt rows until 26 (28,30) sts rem. Work 1 row.

SHAPE SHOULDER

Cast off 7 sts at beg of next row and foll alt row, then 6 (7,8) sts at beg of foll alt row. Work 1 row. Cast off.

Slip next 13 sts onto stitch holder and leave. Join yarn to rem sts and work other side to correspond.

Sleeves

Using 3.00 mm needles and C3, cast on 41 (41,43) sts.

Work 14 rows rib as for Back, inc 8 sts evenly across last row... 49 (49,51) sts.

Change to 3.75 mm needles.

Work 4 rows stocking st.

5th row K2, "M1", knit to last 2 sts, "M1", K2.

Cont in stocking st, inc (as before) at each end of foll 4th rows until there are 65 (67,71) sts.

Work 9 (13,15) rows stocking st.

Change to 4.00 mm needles.

Work rows 1 to 12 incl from Graph A, using C3 instead of C4 and C4 instead of C1.

Change to 3.75 mm needles.

Using C4 for rem, cast off 8 sts at beg of next 6 rows. Cast off rem sts.

Neckband

Using backstitch, join right shoulder seam. With right side facing, using 3.00 mm needles and C3, knit up 69 (75,75) sts evenly around neck, incl sts from stitch holder. Work 21 rows rib as for Back, beg with a 2nd row. Cast off *loosely* in rib.

Make up

With a slightly damp cloth and warm iron, press lightly. Using backstitch, join left shoulder, sleeve and side seams to coloured threads. Sew in sleeves. Fold neckband in half onto wrong side and slipstitch in position. Embroider Satin Stitch bars in contrasting colours on back and front as illustrated. Press seams.

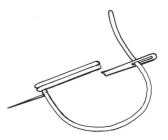

Cardigan

Back

Using 3.00 mm needles and C4, cast on 83 (87,91) sts.

Work 14 rows rib as for Back of Jumper.

Change to 3.75 mm needles.

Work 4 rows stocking st.

Change to 4.00 mm needles.

Note In Fair Isle patt, **do not weave** colours but carry colour not in use *loosely* across on wrong side. It is important, however, that no colour should be carried across more than 7 sts, and where this is necessary it should be woven under and over colour in use at centre st. Always carry colours to ends of rows and always carry C1 above C4. Work rows 1 to 12 incl from Graph B (see page 104).

Change to 3.75 mm needles.

Using C1, work in stocking st until work measures 22.5 (24,25.5) cm from beg, ending with a purl row.

Tie a coloured thread at each end of last row to mark beg of armholes as there is no armhole shaping.

Using C2 for rem, work 48 (50,52) rows stocking st.

SHAPE SHOULDERS

Cast off 7 (7,8) sts at beg of next 4 (6,6) rows, then 7 (8,7) sts at beg of foll 4 (2,2) rows.

Cast off rem 27 (29,29) sts.

Left Front

Using 3.00 mm needles and C4, cast on 41 (43,45) sts.

Work 14 rows rib as for Back, inc once in centre of last row... 42 (44,46) sts.

Change to 3.75 mm needles.

Work 4 rows stocking st.

Change to 4.00 mm needles.

Work rows 1 to 12 incl from Graph B.

Change to 3.75 mm needles.

Using C1, work in stocking st until work measures same as Back to coloured threads, ending with a purl row.

Tie a coloured thread at end of last row to mark beg of armhole.

SHAPE FRONT SLOPE

Using C2 for rem, dec at end of next and alt rows until 37 (39,41) sts rem, then in foll 4th rows until 28 (29,31) sts rem.

Work 3 (1,3) row/s stocking st.

SHAPE SHOULDER

Cast off 7 (7,8) sts at beg of next and alt rows 3 times in all. Work 1 row. Cast off.

Right Front

Work to correspond with Left Front.

Sleeves

Using 3.00 mm needles and C3, cast on 41 (41,43) sts.

Work 14 rows rib as for Back, inc 10 sts evenly across last row... 51 (51,53) sts.

Change to 3.75 mm needles.

Work 4 rows stocking st.

5th row K2, "M1", knit to last 2 sts, "M1", K2.

Cont in stocking st, inc (as before) at each end of alt rows until there are 57 (57,59) sts, then in foll 4th rows until there are 71 (73,75) sts.

Work 5 (9,15) rows stocking st.

Change to 4.00 mm needles.

Work rows 1 to 12 incl from Graph B, using C3 instead of C4 and C4 instead of C1.

Change to 3.75 mm needles.

Using C4 for rem, cast off 8 sts at beg of next 6 rows. Cast off rem sts.

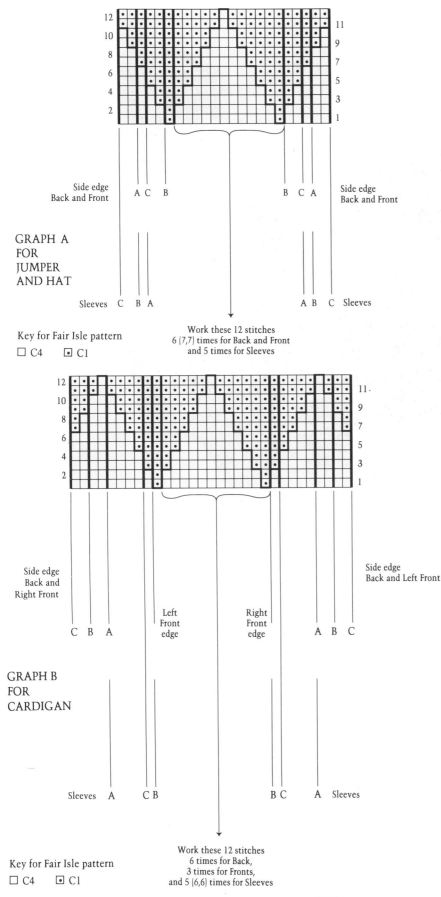

Side edge
Back and Front

A C B

B C A

Side edge
Back and Front

GRAPH A
FOR
JUMPER
AND HAT

Sleeves C B A

A B C Sleeves

Key for Fair Isle pattern

□ C4   ⊡ C1

Work these 12 stitches
6 (7,7) times for Back and Front
and 5 times for Sleeves

Side edge
Back and
Right Front

C B A

Left
Front
edge

Right
Front
edge

Side edge
Back and Left Front

A B C

GRAPH B
FOR
CARDIGAN

Sleeves A   C B

B C   A Sleeves

Key for Fair Isle pattern

□ C4   ⊡ C1

Work these 12 stitches
6 times for Back,
3 times for Fronts,
and 5 (6,6) times for Sleeves

Front Band

Using backstitch, join shoulder seams.
Using 3.00 mm needles and C3, cast
on 11 sts.
Work 4 rows rib as for Back.

FOR BOY

★★★ **5th row**   Rib 4, cast off 2 sts,
rib 5.

6th row   Rib 5, *turn*, cast on 2 sts,
turn, rib 4… buttonhole.

FOR GIRL

★★★ **5th row**   Rib 5, cast off 2 sts,
rib 4.

6th row   Rib 4, *turn*, cast on 2 sts,
turn, rib 5… buttonhole.

FOR BOY OR GIRL

Work 14 (16,16) rows rib. ★★★
Rep from ★★★ to ★★★ 3 times, then
5th and 6th rows once… 5
buttonholes.
Cont without further buttonholes
until band is length required to fit
(slightly stretched) along Fronts and
across Back neck. Cast off in rib.

Make up

With a slightly damp cloth and warm
iron, press lightly. Using backstitch,
join sleeve and side seams to coloured
threads. Sew in sleeves. Sew front band
in position. Sew on buttons. Embroider
Satin Stitch bars (see page 102) in contrasting colours on back and fronts as
illustrated. Press seams.

Hat

Using 3.00 mm needles and C2, cast on 133 (139,145) sts.

Work 27 rows rib as for Back of Jumper (1st row is right side of brim).

Change to 3.75 mm needles.

Using C4, work 4 rows stocking st.

Change to 4.00 mm needles.

Work rows 1 to 12 incl from Graph A (page 104) as for Size B (A,B) of Back.

Change to 3.75 mm needles.

Using C1 for rem, cont in stocking st until work measures 13.5 (14,14.5) cm from centre row of rib, ending with a purl row.

SHAPE TOP

1st row K1, ★ K2 tog, K4, rep from ★ to end.

2nd and alt rows Purl.

3rd row K1, ★ K2 tog, K3, rep from ★ to end.

5th row K1, ★ K2 tog, K2, rep from ★ to end.

7th row K1, ★ K2 tog, K1, rep from ★ to end.

9th row K1, ★ K2 tog, rep from ★ to end... 23 (24,25) sts.

Break off yarn, run end through rem sts, draw up and fasten off *securely*.

Make up

With a slightly damp cloth and warm iron, press lightly. Using backstitch, join seam, reversing for ¾ of rib for brim. Press seam. Using C3, make a pompom (see page 48) and attach to centre of crown. Turn back brim.

Scarf

Using 3.75 mm needles and C3, cast on 35 (35,41) sts.

Knit in garter st until work measures 75 (75,85) cm from beg. Cast off *loosely*. Make fringe (see below) on ends of scarf as illustrated.

FRINGE

Wind yarn round a piece of cardboard 6 cm wide (or desired width) and cut along one edge. With wrong side facing, using crochet hook and two or more strands of yarn (diagram shows 3 strands), fold yarn in half and draw loop through a stitch on garment (A), draw ends through this loop (B), and pull lightly to form knot. Diagram C shows right side of knot.

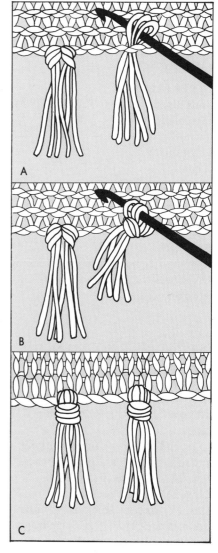

Pat-a-cake

The colourful, lovely motif on the front, back and sleeves of this raglan sleeved jumper is done with knitting stitch embroidery

MEASUREMENTS
This garment is designed to be a generous fit.

Size		A	B	C
Approx age	months	18	24	36
Fits underarm	cm	52.5	55	57.5
	ins	21	22	23
Garment measures	*cm*	*60*	*63*	*66*
Length	cm	31	33	35
Sleeve fits	cm	21	23	25
(or length desired)				

MATERIALS
Patons Bluebell 5 Ply or Patons 5 Ply Machinewash 50 g balls

Main colour (M)	3	3	4
1st contrast (C1)	1	1	1
2nd contrast (C2)	1	1	1
3rd contrast	small quantity for embroidery		

ACCESSORIES
1 pair each 3.75 mm (no. 9) and 3.00 mm (no. 11) Milward knitting needles or sizes needed to give correct tension, 2 stitch holders.

TENSION
26.5 sts to 10 cm in width over stocking st, using 3.75 mm needles.
Please check your tension carefully. If less sts use smaller needles, if more sts use bigger needles.

Back
Using 3.00 mm needles and M, cast on 81 (85,89) sts.
1st row K2, ★ P1, K1, rep from ★ to last st, K1.
2nd row K1, ★ P1, K1, rep from ★ to end.
Rep 1st and 2nd rows 5 times, working 2 rows M, 2 rows C1, 2 rows C2, then 4 rows M... 12 rows rib in all.
Change to 3.75 mm needles.
Using M, work in stocking st until work measures 17.5 (19,20.5) cm from beg, ending with a purl row.

SHAPE ARMHOLES
Cast off 3 sts at beg of next 2 rows.
★★
Working in stocking st stripes of 2 rows each C1 and C2, then rem in M, dec at each end of next and alt rows until 33 (37,41) sts rem, then in every row until 23 sts rem.
Leave rem sts on a stitch holder.

Front
Work as for Back to ★★.
Working in stocking st stripes of 2 rows each C1 and C2, then rem in M,
dec at each end of next and alt rows until 51 (55,57) sts rem.
Work 1 row.

SHAPE NECK
Next row K2 tog, K19 (21,22), *turn* and cont on these 20 (22,23) sts.
Work 1 row.
Dec at armhole edge in next and alt rows 8 (8,7) times in all, **at same time** dec at neck edge in next and foll 4th rows 4 times in all... 8 (10,12) sts.
Dec at armhole edge in every row 5 (7,9) times, **at same time** dec at neck edge in foll 4th row... 2 sts.
Next row P2, *turn*, K2 tog. Fasten off.
Slip next 9 sts onto a stitch holder and leave. Join yarn to rem sts and work other side to correspond.

Sleeves
Using 3.00 mm needles and M, cast on 39 (39,41) sts.
Work 12 rows rib in stripes as for Back, inc 6 (8,6) sts evenly across last row... 45 (47,47) sts.
Change to 3.75 mm needles.
Using M, work 4 rows stocking st.
5th row K2, "M1", knit to last 2 sts, "M1", K2.
Cont in stocking st, inc (as before) at each end of foll 8th (8th,10th) rows until there are 57 (59,59) sts rem, then in foll 10th (10th,12th) row/s until there are 59 (61,61) sts.
Cont without shaping until work measures 21 (23,25) cm (or length desired) from beg, ending with a purl row.

SHAPE RAGLAN
Cast off 3 sts at beg of next 2 rows.
Working in stocking st stripes of 2 rows each C1 and C2, then M for rem, dec at each end of next and alt (*alt*,4th) rows until 7 (7,51) sts rem. **Size C only**, then in alt rows until 7 sts rem.
All sizes, work 1 row. Cast off.

Neckband
Using backstitch, join raglan seams, leaving left back raglan open and noting that tops of Sleeves form part of neckline. With right side facing, using 3.00 mm needles and M, knit

up 89 (93,93) sts evenly around neck, incl sts from stitch holders.

Work 15 rows rib as for Back, beg with a 2nd row and working 2 rows each M, C1, C2, then 9 rows M. Cast off *loosely* in rib.

Make up

With a slightly damp cloth and warm iron, press lightly. Using Knitting Stitch (see page 40) and contrasting colours, embroider motifs from graph (see below) as illustrated. Using back-stitch, join left back raglan, side and sleeve seams. Fold neckband in half onto wrong side and slipstitch in position. Press seams.

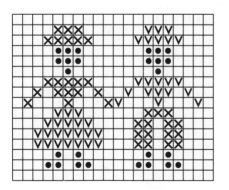

Key for Knitting Stitch embroidery

□ M

⊡ Yellow

☑ Green

☒ Red

Knitting abbreviations

K = knit; **P** = purl; **sl** = slip; **psso** = pass slipped stitch(es) over; **tbl** = through back of loop(s); **y bk** = yarn back — take yarn under needle from purling position into knitting position; **y ft** = yarn front — bring yarn under needle from knitting position into purling position; **y fwd** = yarn forward — bring yarn under needle, then over into knitting position again, thus making a stitch; **yon** = yarn over needle — take yarn over top of needle into knitting position, thus making a stitch; **yrn** = yarn round needle — take yarn right round needle into purling position, thus making a stitch; **"M1"** = make 1 — pick up loop which lies before next stitch, place on left-hand needle and knit (or purl) into back of loop; **garter st** = every row knit; **stocking st** = 1 row knit, 1 row purl; **reverse stocking st** = 1 row purl, 1 row knit (purl side is right side).

When instructions read "Cast off 2 sts, K2" (or similar stitches), the stitch left on the right-hand needle, after casting off, is counted as one stitch.

alt = alternate; **beg** = begin or beginning; **cont** = continue; **dec** = decrease, decreased, decreases or decreasing; **foll** = following or follows; **inc** = increase, increased, increases or increasing; **incl** = including or inclusive; **O** = no rows, stitches or times; **patt** = pattern; **rem** = remain, remains, remainder or remaining; **rep** = repeat; **st, sts** = stitch, stitches; **tog** = together; **cm** = centimetre(s); **mm** = millimetre(s); **ins** = inches.

The first row is always the right side of the work unless otherwise stated.

ACKNOWLEDGEMENTS

The publishers thank the following for their assistance in the photography of this book:

Cuddles
Boutique for children Pagewood, NSW

Hopscotch
for good toys Lindfield, NSW

The Quilting Bee Gordon, NSW

◎Target.

Target Pagewood, NSW

Pattern instructions continued

Bye, baby bunting
continued from page 19

1st and alt rows (wrong side) Knit.

2nd row ★ Inc in next st, K10 (15, 20, 25), inc in next st, rep from ★ once, K1.

4th row ★ Inc in next st, K12 (17, 22, 27), inc in next st, rep from ★ once, K1.

6th row ★ Inc in next st, K14 (19, 24, 29), inc in next st, rep from ★ once, K1.

8th row ★ Inc in next st, K16 (21, 26, 31), inc in next st, rep from ★ once, K1.

10th row ★ Inc in next st, K18 (23, 28, 33), inc in next st, rep from ★ once, K1... 45 (55, 65, 75) sts.

Knit 7 (9, 11, 13) rows garter st.

SHAPE INSTEP
1st row K27 (32, 37, 42), K2 tog, *turn.*

2nd row K10, K2 tog, *turn.*

Rep 2nd row 12 (16, 20, 24) times.

Next row Knit to end... 31 (37, 43, 49) sts.

Next row Knit.

Next row K1, ★ y fwd, K2 tog, K1, rep from ★ to end.

Next row Knit, inc 2 sts evenly across... 33 (39, 45, 51) sts.

Next row K1, ★ P1, K1, rep from ★ to end.

Rep last row 23 times. Cast off *loosely* in moss st.

Make up
With a slightly damp cloth and warm iron, press lightly, taking care not to flatten patt. Using a flat seam, join leg and foot seams. Thread ribbon through holes at ankle.

Hush-a-bye baby
continued from page 22

Neckband
Using backstitch, join shoulder seams. With right side facing and using 2.75 mm needles, knit up 85 (93, 99, 99) sts evenly around neck, incl sts from stitch holders.

1st row K5, ★ P1, K1, rep from ★ to last 4 sts, K4.

2nd row K6, ★ P1, K1, rep from ★ to last 5 sts, K2, y fwd, K2 tog, K1.

Rep 1st and 2nd rows once, omitting buttonhole.

Cast off 5 sts at beg of next 2 rows.

Work 4 rows rib. Cast off *loosely* in rib.

Make up
With a slightly damp cloth and warm iron, press lightly. Using backstitch, join side and sleeve seams. Sew in sleeves. Fold neckband in half onto wrong side and slipstitch in position. Sew underlap in position. Sew on buttons. Press seams.

Tommy Snooks and Bessy Brooks
continued from page 51

rib 4... 5 buttonholes. Work 3 rows rib. Cast off *loosely* in rib.

Right Front Band for boy or Left Front Band for girl
Work as for other band, omitting buttonholes.

Make up
With a slightly damp cloth and warm iron, press lightly, taking care not to flatten patt. Using backstitch, join sleeve and side seams to coloured threads. Sew in sleeves. Fold neckband in half onto wrong side and slipstitch in position. Sew front bands in position, sewing through both thicknesses of neckband. Sew on buttons. Press seams.

Curly locks, curly locks
continued from page 56

Make up
With a slightly damp cloth and warm iron, press lightly, taking care not to flatten patt. Using backstitch, join side and sleeve seams. Sew ends of front bands in position. Sew on buttons. Press seams.

Little Tommy Tittlemouse
continued from page 66

With right side facing, rejoin yarn and knit up 5 sts evenly along edge of 5 rows of heel, knit across 17 (17, 19, 19, 19) sts of heel, knit up 5 sts evenly along edge of heel... 27 (27, 29, 29, 29) sts.

Next row Purl.

SHAPE SIDE OF INSTEP
1st row K1, sl 1, K1, psso, knit to last 3 sts, K2 tog, K1.

2nd row Purl.
Rep 1st and 2nd rows 4 times...
17(17,19,19,19) sts.
Work a further 10 (14,16,18,20) rows stocking st.

SHAPE TOE
1st row K2, sl 1, K1, psso, knit to last 4 sts, K2 tog, K2.
2nd row Purl.
Rep 1st and 2nd rows 1 (1,2,2,2) time/s, then 1st row once... 11 sts.
Cast off.

Make up
Do not press. Using a flat seam, join cast-off sts tog at toe. Using backstitch join foot and centre back seams.

Oranges and lemons
continued from page 68

Work 7 rows rib as before, beg with a 2nd row and working a buttonhole (as before) in 4th row.
Cast off *loosely* in rib.

Make up
With a slightly damp cloth and warm iron, press lightly. Using backstitch, join sleeve and side seams to coloured threads. Sew in sleeves. Sew on buttons. Press seams.

Friday's child
continued from page 83

Right Front Band
Work as for Left Front Band, omitting buttonholes.

Make up
With a slightly damp cloth and

---

warm iron, press lightly, taking care not to flatten patt. Using backstitch, join sleeve and side seams to coloured threads. Sew in sleeves. Sew front bands in position. Sew underlap in position. Sew on buttons. Press seams.

Mary, Mary
continued from page 86

Neckband
Using backstitch, join shoulder seams. Sew Front Bands in position. With right side facing, using 3.00 mm needle holding Right Front Band sts and M, knit up 69 (75,79) sts evenly around neck, then rib across Left Front Band sts... 87 (93,97) sts.
Work 8 rows rib as for Back, beg with a 2nd row and working a buttonhole (as before) in 4th row.
Cast off 9 sts in rib at beg of next 2 rows.
Work 7 rows rib. Cast off *loosely* in rib.

Make up
With a slightly damp cloth and warm iron, press lightly. Using backstitch, join sleeve and side seams to coloured threads. Sew in sleeves. Fold neckband in half onto wrong side and slipstitch in position. Sew on buttons. Embroider as illustrated — we used Lazy Daisy Stitch for the petals and leaves, French Knots for the flower centres and Chain Stitch for the flower stems and bows. Use 1, 2 or 3 strands of yarn to give the desired effect — the more strands, the stronger the colour will be. Press seams.

Peter Piper
continued from page 92

Sleeves
Using 3.25 mm needles, cast on 35 (35,37) sts.
Work 12 rows rib as for Back, inc 9 sts evenly across last row... 44 (44,46) sts.
Change to 4.00 mm needles.
1st and 3rd rows Knit.
2nd and 4th rows K10 (10,11), P6, K12, P6, K10 (10,11).
Keeping patt correct as for Back, *as placed* in last 4 rows, and working extra sts into patt, inc at each end of next and foll 6th rows until there are 56 (56,54) sts, then in foll 8th rows until there are 60 (62,64) sts.
Cont without shaping until work measures 19 (21,23) cm (or 2 cm less than length desired to allow for loose fit) from beg, working last row on wrong side.
Keeping patt correct, cast off 8 sts at beg of next 6 rows.
Cast off rem sts.

Neckband
Using backstitch, join right shoulder seam. With right side facing and using 3.25 mm needles, knit up 83 (89,89) sts evenly around neck, dec once in centre of Front stitch holder and 2 sts evenly across Back stitch holder.
Work 15 rows rib as for Back, beg with a 2nd row.
Cast off *loosely* in rib.

Make up
With a slightly damp cloth and warm iron, press lightly, taking care not to flatten patt. Using backstitch, join left shoulder, sleeve and side seams to coloured threads. Sew in sleeves. Fold neckband in half onto wrong side and slipstitch in position. Press seams.

This edition published in 1995 by Leopard Books
Random House, 20 Vauxhall Bridge Road,
London SW1V 2SA

First published in 1992 by Murdoch Books®, a division of Murdoch Magazines Pty Ltd,
in association with Coats Patons Handknitting

ISBN 0 7529 0087 0

Pattern Designers and Writers: Maureen Hurley and June McIntyre
Photography: Stuart Spence
Craft Consultant: Lisa Johnson
Art Direction and Design: Michele Withers

Typeset by Post Typesetters, Brisbane
Produced by Mandarin Offset, Hong Kong